Modern Childrearing:

A Behavioral Approach

UNIVERSITY OF MARYLAND
University Counseling Center
Shoemaker Building
College Park, Maryland 20742

Modern Childrearing:

A Behavioral Approach

Donald K. Pumroy
Shirley S. Pumroy

Nelson-Hall nh Chicago

Library of Congress Cataloging in Publication Data

Pumroy, Donald Keith, 1925-
  Modern childrearing.

  Bibliography: p.
  Includes index.
  1. Children — Management. 2. Child psychology.
I. Pumroy, Shirley Ann Spence, 1928-   joint author.
II. Title.
HQ769.P843   649′.1   77-26964
ISBN 0-88229-185-8

Manufactured in the United States of America

10 9 8 7 6 5 4 3 2 1

Contents

Preface

W e have been involved in a behavioral approach to child-rearing for a number of years. While it is difficult to pin down the beginning, we were both fortunate enough to do our doctoral research under the direction of Dr. Sidney Bijou at the University of Washington. This consisted of a learning problem using nursery-school children as subjects. While the focus was on learning principles, this experience was most helpful to us later in the application of these principles to everyday life situations. A few years after receiving our Ph.Ds, we had a baby boy and then a girl. In the day-to-day interactions with the children, we found ourselves confronted with a variety of child-rearing problems. As we tried to find solutions, we discovered that the problems lent themselves to experimental analysis, and we felt a solution might be based on learning principles.

One problem consisted of our boy waking up early in the morning, and in turn, waking up the rest of the family. Using learning principles, this problem was analyzed, solved, and its solution subsequently published. As other problems presented themselves, they too were treated and solved with this approach. It appeared that the problems we faced were not unique and we thought that perhaps this approach would help other parents. In 1964, Don applied for and was awarded a grant from the National Institute of Mental Health to do just that. The basic outline of this book was established at that time. Since that time other activities (e.g., teaching child psychology, working with parents and teachers, serving as director of research at the University of Maryland Nursery School, working as a psychologist for Maryland Council of Parent Participation Nursery Schools, experiences with behavior service consultants, functioning as director of the School Psychology Program at the University of Maryland) have helped in improving, adding to, and modifying the material.

There are a variety of people who have had an influence on our thinking. The approach followed is one developed by B. F. Skinner. Sidney Bijou not only directed our thesis but, more recently, has been most helpful through his writing and research. Other individuals with whom we discussed problems and from whom we've learned would include Allan Leventhal, Charles Ferster, and Leo Walder. So many students have also contributed that it would be difficult to name them all. Certainly Sue Garner, Ralph Holt, Bruce Hutchison, Marilyn McGilvrey, Jenny Steinmetz, and Sharon Wallace stand out. This book, consequently, is the fruition of all these interactions and experiences.

We hope this book will serve two purposes. One is as a supplemental text for child psychology courses, since it is based on clearly defined psychological principles and many examples are included from everyday child-rearing experiences. A glossary is provided at the end of the book to help the reader understand the terms. The second purpose is to provide parents with principles and techniques that will help them understand their child's behavior and provide a way to change that behavior. Because the book is designed to serve two functions, it is divided into two parts. The first part is an explanation of the approach and the principles involved. The second part consists of studies that have applied these principles to particular child-rearing problems which have confronted parents. It was not easy to find appropriate studies, studies that presented "normal" parents dealing with "normal" children solving everyday problems. Historically, research has been more concerned with the disturbed child and the well-known investigators in the field have studied retarded and autistic children primarily. Of late more "normal" studies have been conducted. The studies are not particularly complex and illustrate clearly the various points made in the first section. As the principles stated are also applicable to problems found in the classroom, teachers will, one hopes, find this book useful.

In contrast to other child-rearing books, we hope to be quite specific about what a parent should do to change a child's behavior. We have tried to be most explicit. Notice that we have not taken a stand on what is the correct or desired behavior of the child; that is left to the parent to decide. Behavior perceived as appropriate in one family may be viewed as inappropriate in another. From our experience we feel that parents usually have the child's best interest at heart; the difficulty is that parents frequently do not know how to cope with a child's behavior. They may try various ways to change the behavior, but if these are not successful they become frustrated, and once frustrated, may become emotional and punish the child. This, in turn, is even more destructive to the parent-child relationship and the problem is magnified. If the parents did know how to change their child's behavior, the problem could possibly be eliminated or reduced in a short time.

Perhaps the attempt to have the book serve two functions (supplemental textbook and a book on child-rearing) is not as unusual as it may seem at first. As more and more people attend college, the level of sophistication rises so that the two functions cited above can be handled at the same level of content. Secondly, many of the students taking child psychology will take no other psychology courses and have as one of their strong interests learning how to be a better parent. It is our hope that such will be the case.

We would like to thank Joe Matarazzo for his support with the book and our editor, Mr. E. P. Epler. Ms. Linda Hall and Mrs. Irma Nicholson typed the manuscript and their effort is much appreciated.

Chapter 1

Introduction

Mrs. Roberts has a problem with her two children, John, age ten, and Betty, eight. She says that they always argue about the most insignificant things. Their arguments then get louder and John usually hits Betty who runs crying to Mrs. Roberts. Mrs. Roberts usually tries to find out who was responsible for the argument and then punishes the guilty one. The punishment sometimes means spending an hour in his or her room. When this has taken place in the past, the guilty child has played the record player or read, so it didn't seem like much punishment. Lately, because the punishment has seemed ineffective, Mrs. Roberts has had her husband spank the guilty child when he gets home, but he is somewhat reluctant to do this and it only happened three times. The arguments between the children have continued and seem even worse than before.

The problem these parents face is not unique. In fact, it has probably taken place in one form or another in every family that has two or more children. Parents and child experts have attempted to cope with such problems in a variety of ways. From a review of various child experts, it can be seen that there are several threads of similarity in their approaches. One point of agreement is that the child has a certain amount of aggression that must be released in some fashion. Thus, if the child were given a chance to hit a punching bag, or indulge in some strenuous exercise, there would be a reduction in his or her aggression

1

and, consequently, fewer arguments. Others state that children should be reasoned with; by this they mean that a child should be talked to and the mother should explain to the child that he or she should not argue. Another view is that the child should discuss his feelings, giving him a chance to ventilate them. The parent could or should help a child label his or her feelings with statements such as, "You are feeling angry."

THE BEHAVIORAL APPROACH TO CHILD PROBLEMS

The difference between the behavioral approach and the more traditional view is that the former focuses strictly on the child's behavior. It is not concerned with any inner self or needs but it is concerned with a precise definition of the behavior considered a problem by the parent. Thus, in the situation cited earlier, the behavior of concern was the constant arguing of the children. If that behavior could be eliminated, the problem would be solved. The problem then is the behavior of concern. We realize that this view is initially difficult to conceptualize. Probably the main reason for this difficulty is that it is contrary to the way people in our culture have been taught to think about others. To think only in terms of behavior has a cold, sterile, impersonal flavor that makes it somewhat repulsive to individuals. Logically, though, one must admit that when the behavior of concern is eliminated, the parent is happier. So is the child. Perhaps the reader could follow this position more easily if he or she views the behaviorist approach as a new, separate, or different view and holds the traditional in reserve while learning about behaviorism.

There are several ways in which the two approaches differ:

1. *The behavioral view is concerned with behavior only* and not with the inner state of the child. The child is not thought of as shy, aggressive, incorrigible, dishonest, and so forth. The focus, instead, is on the *behavior* of the child which is viewed as a problem by the parents, e.g., hitting another child, crying and whining, not eating a good breakfast, teasing, not going to bed on time, and wetting one's pants. It is apparent that in the behavioral approach the problem is clearly defined and easily communicated. Words such as "shy" or "aggressive" are not precise in meaning and may have different connotations for different individuals. The precision of the behavioral phrases is evident; a person knows clearly what is meant by "hitting another child" and it has the added virtue of not labeling the child with a negative attribute.

2. The behavioral approach states that *the behavior of concern is the problem.* The traditional view states that the child is disturbed (insane, upset, emotionally unstable, neurotic) and because of this disturbance, his behavior is deviant. To help this child, one should treat the disturbance, not the behavior. The traditionalist believes the inner self is something like a hydraulic system; the

elimination of a deviant behavior will cause a back-up in the system and a new and different deviancy will manifest itself. Thus, if a child is stopped from thumb-sucking, he will start to wet the bed. If the bed-wetting is eliminated, he may begin to fondle himself. If that behavior is stopped, he might start to stutter, and so on. This relationship between different behaviors is referred to as symptom substitution—as one behavior (symptom) is removed, another is substituted. There is some controversy as to whether or not this actually takes place, but enough evidence has been accumulated to indicate that symptom substitution is not an *inevitable* consequence of the removal of an undesired behavior. If such substitution does take place (and it is questionable), the behaviorist would then be concerned with the new, undesired behavior until it, too, was removed.

3. The two approaches differ in *the cause of a behavior*. Cause, in the traditional view, is some event that has taken place earlier in the life of the person showing the deviant behavior. Some time ago the cause of a deviant behavior was thought to be a particular traumatic event. The reader may recall the book and movie entitled *The Three Faces Of Eve* in which the split personality presented was caused by having to kiss her dead grandmother. Cause then is almost always related to some earlier traumatic event.

In the behavioral approach, cause is attributed to the events that follow a certain behavior. What follows the behavior is responsible for causing the behavior to be repeated. Perhaps an example from laboratory work with children will clarify this point. A box was built with two holes (one above the other) so that when a ball was dropped in the top hole, it would emerge from the bottom hole. Also, on the right side of the box was a small plastic dish. The inside of the box was so constructed that when the ball was dropped in the top hole, a piece of candy or toy would fall into the plastic dish, and the ball would then emerge from the bottom hole. The ball could then be dropped again. If a child were introduced to this apparatus and allowed to drop the ball in the top hole, a piece of candy would fall into the plastic dish. He or she would then, in all likelihood, pick up the ball and drop it in the box again. If the child were given another piece of candy, he or she would probably continue to drop the ball again and again. What, then is the cause of the ball-dropping behavior? According to the behaviorists, the candy that follows the ball-dropping behavior is the cause of that behavior. There are many examples from everyday life. Temper tantrums persist because the child gets what he or she wants following such behavior. The child practices diligently on the piano because, following such behavior, his mother tells him how well he plays. More will be presented on this principle in later chapters. One positive aspect of the behavioral approach is that it tends to make parents who are having problems with their children feel less guilty. As anyone working with parents will recount, frequently parents berate themselves severely when their child shows some deviant behavior. Such questions as, "Where did I go wrong?" are commonplace. The behaviorists' answer to this question is that that is really not too important, because there is no way of going back in time and changing what has been done. The important point is what can be done today or tomorrow to change or eliminate the undesirable behavior.

4. Another area of difference is the *individual upon whom the treatment is focused*. In traditional work with children who are having problems, it is frequently the child who is treated. The treatment will vary depending upon the age of the child and the orientation of the person doing the treatment. The child may be treated with a variety of play-therapy techniques or may be treated, if older, as an adult in some sort of talking therapy. The parents are quite often required to participate in a therapeutic relationship. With some experts, the parents are seen alone and in other cases the whole family is involved.

The behaviorist is most likely to work only with the parents and not with the child. The behavioral position is that the parents have to be taught the best way to change their child so that he or she will show more of the desirable behavior and less of the undesirable. One reason for working with the parents and not the child is that the therapist has only one hour, two at the most, per week to have an impact on the child while the parents have many hours. Another advantage is that the responsibility for the child's behavior remains with the parents and the parents cannot place that responsibility on the therapist. It seems logical that treatment be given in this way, legally, because parents are almost exclusively responsible for their children. The assumption that parents know what is best for their child also seems to be helpful to the parents.

While the differences between the traditional and behavioral approaches have been stressed, there are also similarities. These are particularly evident when a child expert is working with a parent concerned about his or her child. Suggestions and guidance given by a traditional child therapist are very frequently focused on the child's behavior. The traditionalist, however, still perceives the cause as lying buried somewhere in the child's past. The behaviorist, on the other hand, believes that if the behavior is changed, the problem is solved.

SUMMARY

The behavioral approach to children's problems was discussed and compared to the traditional view. The behavioral approach focuses on the behavior of concern. Concepts such as problem and cause were defined in behavioral terms. In this approach the behavior of concern *is* the problem; the events that follow the behavior of concern *are* the cause. Treatment employing the behavioral approach is more likely to be carried out with the parents than with the child.

Chapter 2

Defining and Measuring Behavior

I t should be obvious by now that the key word in this book is *behavior*. More precisely it is the child's behavior that is considered a problem to parents or teachers (as the teachers, in turn, make problems for the parent). Because the problem is defined by the individual parents, a behavior that is viewed as a problem by one set of parents may not be viewed as such by another. Some parents, for example, are more concerned with cleanliness than others. Some parents want their children to be more aggressive than others and, consequently, they are more concerned when their children do not stand up for their rights.

REACHING AGREEMENT ON THE PROBLEM

It is very important that both the mother and father work together in changing their children's behavior. Some agreement must be reached as to whether or not the behavior is a problem recognized by *both* parents. If the parents do not agree, the situation is much more complex and success is less likely. In some cases, it may be necessary to compromise in order to reach agreement. One couple seen by us was concerned about their little girl's eating behavior. The problem was complex because the mother felt that overeating was desirable because she associated it with good health. The father, on the other hand, as well as the child's pediatrician, thought the child was overweight. Much time and effort had

5

to be spent with the mother and father to reach a compromise on the child's eating behavior. Had not such a compromise been made, however, it would have been difficult, if not impossible, to resolve this problem.

Once agreement is reached, the parents should make sure that the behavior is clearly defined. It may take some time and discussion to define the behavior, but the time spent at this point is worthwhile and will reduce problems later. Some behaviors are more easily defined than others. Thumb-sucking and bed-wetting are fairly obvious. If the child's thumb is in her mouth, she is thumb-sucking. If the bed is wet in the morning, the child wet the bed. Other behaviors are not so obvious and may require some care in their definition. Take the problem of the child not doing homework. How does the parent know if homework was assigned? If the child attempts to do the homework, is that a satisfactory solution to the parent? If he spends a certain amount of time at his homework, is that satisfactory? Does his homework have to be perfect to be acceptable? These and other questions obscure the definition of the behavior. With more ambiguous behaviors, reliance must be placed on someone's judgment. The more objective and clear the definition, however, the greater the likelihood of success in changing the behavior.

EXERCISE: DEFINING THE PROBLEM

Practice on some of these behaviors by giving precise definitions and thinking of problems that might arise where there would be disagreement:

1. Running into the street
2. Crying, whining behavior
3. Teasing a younger sibling
4. Making one's bed

ADVANTAGES OF BEHAVIORAL DEFINITION

As a person begins to think in behavioral terms, he or she will notice two aspects of this conceptualization. One is that the communication about a child's problems is much clearer. It is more precise to say that a child sucks his thumb than that the child is insecure; to say that a child stands in the corner and does not interact with his peers than to say he is shy. In short, communication can be effected in a more precise manner.

Another observation one might make is that the solution is more apparent. To cure a child of shyness seems a difficult and complex problem. Where does one start? To help a child move away from the corner and interact with peers is a much more approachable and potentially solvable problem.

DETERMINING FREQUENCY OF BEHAVIOR

The person who can think in terms of precise behavior may also notice a very important dimension in this approach. That is, we can keep track of how often the behavior takes place — the frequency of the behavior. The frequency determines whether or not the behavior has reached the proportions of a problem. The problem may be the absence of a particular behavior. Examples would be: saying "please" and "thank you," carrying out trash, talking, washing the dishes, and so forth. At the other extreme, the parent may be concerned about an undesirable behavior of the child that takes place quite frequently, e.g., bed-wetting, using dirty words, hitting, and crying.

It should be noted that the reason the child is labeled with some inner-state word in the first place is because of the behavior he or she displays. The mother's concern about her child's shyness can be translated into her concern about the child's behaviors of staying by himself and not interacting with others. The "shyness" is only a problem to the mother because the behaviors mentioned take place too often. The "aggressive" child is labeled so because of behavior in which he *frequently* hits others, pushes, shoves, and yells.

RECORDING FREQUENCY OF BEHAVIOR

The next step is to consider how a parent can keep track of the frequency of a behavior over a period of time. It is important to do this for two reasons. The first is that a parent, after keeping data for a while, can determine the seriousness of the problem. A behavior, initially thought to be a problem by the parent, may turn out to be relatively unimportant when its frequency is recorded and observed. In some cases a behavior that is very emotionally upsetting to a parent (e.g., serious temper tantrums) may at first seem to be a problem but cease to be so when it is observed that it takes place rarely.

Another reason for recording the frequency of a behavior is that the parent can measure the effect of different techniques by observing the increase or decrease in frequency of the behavior in much the same way as a weight watcher records his or her weight on a regular basis to determine the effectiveness of different diets.

DIARY-RECORDING METHOD

There are several ways to record the behavioral frequency. One of the most obvious is to record, in a diary fashion, exactly when the behavior took place. An advantage to this is that other important information is usually recorded along with the behavior. An example of a diary by a mother concerned about her son's homework is:

When Bobby came home, he said he had twenty arithmetic problems to do for homework. I didn't say that he had better get started as I've done before. Later that evening, about 7:15, he started his work. He quit at 7:30 to watch TV and I still didn't say anything. That was all he did. The next day I checked his work before he went to school. He had completed eleven problems and they were all correct.

Not only was the frequency of the behavior recorded in the diary (he had done eleven out of twenty problems), but also the mother's reaction to it and her behavior.

Using the diary-recording method, the frequency of behavior can then be plotted on a graph and observed over a period of time. The frequency of the boy's homework behavior could be plotted as in Figure 1.

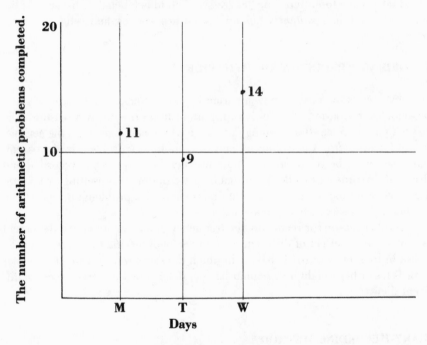

Figure 1. The number of arithmetic problems done each day by Bob (twenty problems done each day).

If Bobby were given twenty arithmetic problems on Monday, Tuesday, and

Wednesday and on Monday he did eleven, nine on Tuesday and fourteen on Wednesday, a graph of his work could be presented. See Figure 1.

TALLY-RECORDING METHOD

There are several other ways to record data. Probably the simplest method is a tally method. Here the behavior is precisely defined (as is always the case) and when it occurs, a mark is simply made on a sheet of paper. The paper may be divided into days although other periods of time may be used. If bed-wetting were the problem, a parent could tape a sheet of paper near the child's bed. Then by each date a W for wet or a D for dry could be easily recorded. An example of

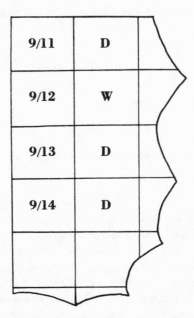

Figure 2. Example of sheet-recording whether child was wet (W) or dry (D) on arising for particular days.

such a tally sheet is presented in Figure 2. In some situations, it may be necessary to use a small card divided into dates when one is attempting to record behavior that is not confined to a particular room or area. A portable recording sheet would have to be used if one were recording such behavior as thumb-sucking, temper tantrums, and shouting. Some parents have used other devices to record behavior, such as a golf-scorer tally that can be worn on the wrist.

EVENT RECORDER

A much more complex way of recording behavior, one used in laboratories where children are studied, is an event recorder. This consists of a roll of paper unrolled at a constant speed by a motor. A pen is mounted above it and draws a line as the paper unrolls. The pen has two positions and can be moved by pressing a lever; if the lever is depressed, it is in one position; if it is not depressed, it is in the other. A person can record a particular behavior by depressing the lever and holding it down as long as the behavior continues and then releasing it as soon as the behavior stops. Since the speed at which the paper unrolls is known, one can measure the length of time the behavior takes place. If one were interested in recording thumb-sucking in this manner and the necessary equipment were available, one would watch the child and depress the lever when the child put his thumb in his mouth and hold it down as long as the thumb stayed in the mouth. An example of such a recording is presented in Figure 3.

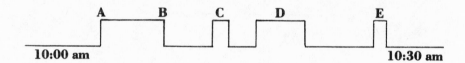

Figure 3. Event recording of a behavior.

The diagram shows us that the observation started at ten o'clock and lasted for thirty minutes. At point A, the child started to suck his thumb and at point B, he removed it from his mouth. On three other occasions (C, D, E) he put his thumb in his mouth for varying amounts of time. There are several pieces of information that can be obtained from such a record: (1) length of observation (thirty minutes); (2) frequency of behavior (four occasions); (3) length of time behavior took place (measure distance between A and B, also C, D, and E and convert to time); (4) ratio of length of time behavior took place to total observation time (the sum found in (3) divided by thirty minutes); and (5) at what time during the observation period the behavior took place (inspection of record). This method is usually restricted to the laboratory and is presented here because of its usefulness in explaining some behavior problems that will be presented later. Much more information is revealed by the event recorder than the tally method. The event recorder produces data that coincide precisely with the behavior in time. The tally method does not tell precisely when the behavior took place nor its duration.

TIME-BLOCK METHOD

The third method is the time-block method. It is halfway between the other two approaches in terms of accurately reflecting the behavior. In this method, a recording sheet is prepared with a series of blocks either in a row or vertically. Each block represents a unit of time. The task of the recorder is to observe the child and if the behavior of concern takes place during that unit of time he will so indicate in that particular block. Data on thumb-sucking might be recorded in the minute blocks as presented in Figure 4. To interpret the above recording, one would notice that the behavior was observed for fifteen minutes. For six minutes, the child had his thumb in his mouth (indicated by T) or during nine minutes of the period observed, the child did not have his thumb in his mouth—

10:00   **10:05**   **10:10**   **10:15**

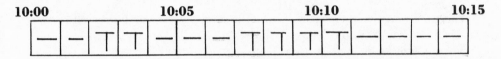

Figure 4. Time-block recording of thumb sucking.

indicated by a minus sign. Even though this child may have sucked his thumb for only a two-second interval, it would be recorded as if the child had sucked his thumb for the full minute. In this sense the event-recording method is much more precise.

This time-block method is flexible because the amount of time per block can be made larger or smaller depending on the behavior observed. The recording paper can then be mounted on a portable clipboard. The time-block technique has been used in a variety of situations, such as recording disruptive behavior in a classroom.

PLOTTING FREQUENCY OF BEHAVIOR

Using any of the four methods described above, the next step consists of plotting the frequency of the behavior over time. It is important to plot the data in order to tell how serious the problem is initially, and also to give an indication of the effectiveness of any technique used to bring about a change.

On the vertical axis, the number of times or frequency of the behavior is recorded; along the horizontal line, time—minutes, hours, days—is plotted. Whether or not a child wet his bed could be plotted. Along the bottom axis would be the number of days and on the vertical axis would be a 1 (wet) or 0 (dry) as appropriate. Homework might be plotted the same way though it is apt to become more complicated. It is important to measure daily the ratio of amount of homework assigned that had been correctly completed over the amount of homework assigned. Some homework assignments lend themselves more easily to such quantification. Thus, a mother can look at certain arithmetic problems done by her child and tell at a glance how many problems were completed and how many were correct. Spelling is equally easy. The assignment of reading a passage in a book or writing a theme is more difficult to assess. Parents should be aware of certain ambiguities in the frequency of the desired behavior and make judgments on the percentage of work accomplished as best they can.

ANALYZING A PROBLEM BEHAVIOR

There are many problems parents observe everyday that can be viewed behaviorally. Perhaps it would be worthwhile to present a problem and then discuss how it might be defined, recorded, and plotted.

Problem: Sarah is seven years old. She will make her bed only if her mother stands over her until the task is completed. Consequently, on some mornings her bed is made while on other days it is not. Her mother is furious when it is not made. *Definition of behavior:* her mother must decide whether the bed is made

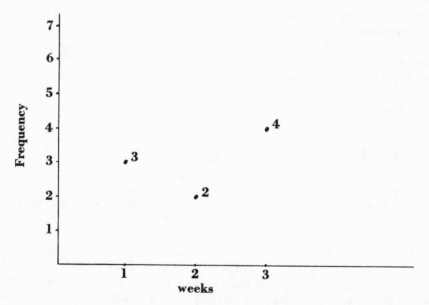

Figure 5. Number of mornings Sarah made her bed per week.

to her satisfaction; if she decides that it is, the behavior of concern has taken place; if not, then it hasn't. For example, it is possible that Sarah might straighten her bed without actually making it. *Recording the behavior:* Because this particular event may or may not take place each day, a chart with the days listed will serve as a recording chart. A sheet of lined paper with a date and space to put a Y for yes, she made her bed or an N for no are sufficient. A calendar could also be used. If Sarah made her bed, her mother could put a Y on that date; if she didn't make her bed, an N. It is important to have a mark for both possibilities so that one doesn't confuse forgetting to record with one of the categories. If one originally decided to put an X in the space if she made her bed and to leave the space blank if she didn't, the mother could possibly forget to record one day, and it would look as if Sarah hadn't made her bed.

Plotting of data: After several weeks of recording Sarah's bed-making behavior, her mother would be able to plot the severity of the problem. One way of doing so would be to plot the number of times she makes her bed per week as indicated in Figure 5.

The hypothetical graph indicates that Sarah made her bed for three mornings the first week, two mornings the second week, and four mornings the third week.

EXERCISES: ANALYZING PROBLEM BEHAVIOR

Analyze the problems presented below in the same fashion as Sarah's bed-making behavior. Remember there are three parts to be discussed: (1) definition of the behavior of concern; (2) recording it; and (3) plotting the data.

1. Johnny is nine years old and has been taking violin lessons for almost a year. In the beginning he practiced each day, but with the coming of spring he has taken to playing outdoors more. His parents are concerned with his lack of practice.

2. Bobby is five years old. His mother has been concerned about his not eating vegetables for some time. Almost every meal when vegetables are served, there is a squabble between Bobby and his mother. She has tried ignoring him, punishing him, scolding him, all to no avail.

3. Betty is three years old. She has been described as spoiled by those that have come in contact with her. More specifically this label seems to mean that whatever Betty wants, Betty gets. If she doesn't get what she wants, she will throw herself on the floor, scream, kick, and sometimes pound her head on the floor. When she does this, her mother gives in to Betty and gives her what she wants or allows her to do what she desires. Her parents are concerned about these temper tantrums.

SUMMARY

This chapter explored ways of defining and measuring behaviors of concern. The importance of a clear definition of the problem in behavioral terms was stressed and illustrated as well as the necessity for agreement between the parents on the problem's definition and desired future behavior. The extent of the problem depends on the frequency of the behavior; various methods for recording frequency of the behavior were discussed: the diary, the tally, the event recorder, and the time-block method. Plotting frequency of behavior over time is an important part of the technique because it indicates the seriousness of the problem as well as the effectiveness of the treatment.

Chapter 3

Increasing the Frequency of Behaviors

If one were to observe and record a child's behavior throughout his waking day, it would soon be apparent that most of the time the child was doing what was acceptable to his or her parents. Wolking (1968) has shown that when a child's behavior is analyzed in this way even a disturbed child displays much normal behavior. A close look at such a detailed analysis, however, might show a parent that there were certain desirable behaviors that *did not take place* and this frequently is the cause of friction. In other cases the friction is brought about by behavior that takes place far too often as far as the parents are concerned. Look at the situations described below and notice that in each case the child's failure to perform a single behavior or his persistent behavior has led to the difficulty.

1. Charles's father has charged him with the responsibility of bringing in the trash cans after the sanitation department leaves them on the parkway. This happens twice a week. Charles frequently forgets to bring them in. His father has become upset on occasion and once refused to take Charlie to a baseball game which he had promised. On another occasion, the father sent Charlie to his room without dinner because he had forgotten.

2. Eddie frequently makes fun of and teases his sister, Betty. If Betty asks her mother how her dress looks, Eddie will say it looks terrible. If she asks for help with her homework, Eddie will say she is too dumb to do it. When she was trying to practice saying a poem for a school activities day, Eddie said she wasn't doing it right. When this happens, Betty usually starts to cry and runs to her mother. Her mother has scolded Eddie for teasing her and is afraid Betty will lose her self-confidence.

3. Mary has difficulty getting up in the morning. Her mother has to awaken her several times. Mary frequently goes without breakfast and her mother has had to drive her to school twice so that she would not be late. The mother yells and nags a great deal every morning.

4. Jerry is assigned homework about two or three times a week. He almost always forgets to do his homework until time to go to bed or until he is ready to leave for school. His parents then become upset because he is either deprived of sleep or doesn't have time for breakfast. His parents practically do his home-work for him so he will be able to sleep or finish his breakfast.

5. Johnny, who is four, received a drum for Christmas. The drum was his favorite toy and he played it almost incessantly. Johnny's father, who is a somewhat tense person, wanted Johnny to spend his time doing something less noisy.

In each of the above situations, it is the lack of a certain behavior, or the performance of a particular behavior that is responsible for a minor family catastrophe. There would, no doubt, be much greater family happiness if, somehow, the parents had at their disposal a technique that would alter behaviors of concern.

POSITIVE REINFORCEMENT

One technique derived from psychological studies for increasing the frequency of behavior is positive reinforcement. This technique relates the behavior of concern to some consequence. If these two, the behavior and the consequence, are paired over a period of time and there is an increase in the frequency of behavior, this phenomena is called positive reinforcement. An example from the laboratory situation mentioned earlier will make the concept clearer. A piece of equipment was designed as follows: a large wooden box had two holes in it, one above the other. If a ball were placed in the top hole, it would roll through the box and come out at the bottom hole. At the side of the box was a small chute connected to a plastic tray. The inside of the box was so arranged that a small piece of candy (M&Ms) would fall down the chute and land in the tray whenever the ball was dropped in the top hole. A diagram of the box is presented in Figure 6. If a child were brought into the room and the apparatus explained, he or she would drop the ball in the upper hole. A piece of candy would fall into the tray and the ball would then emerge from the bottom hole ready to be dropped again. Figure 7 diagrams the above events using the event recorder. (A) indi-

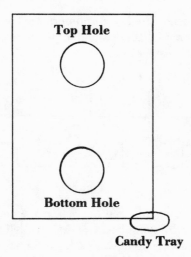

Figure 6. Apparatus to show positive reinforcement.

cates the behavior of concern, the dropping of the ball, and (B) indicates the consequence, the delivery of candy. If the child is left in front of the box, he or she more than likely will pick up the ball again and drop it in the upper hole. If each time he does that a piece of candy is dropped into the tray, there will be an increase in the frequency of dropping the ball in the upper hole. This could be diagrammed as follows:

Notice how the marks that indicate ball-dropping grow closer together as we move to the right. This means that there is either less time between his ball-dropping behavior or that there is an increase in the frequency of his behavior. This procedure is referred to as positive reinforcement. There are several features worth noting about this example:

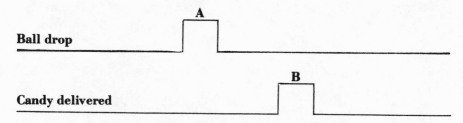

Figure 7. Diagram of positive reinforcement example.

1. The behavior was something the child was *capable* of doing. The task of ball-dropping was an easy one.

2. The consequence used was *appropriate*. The child desired the candy. Had mud pellets been used, there would more than likely have been no increase in the frequency of behavior.

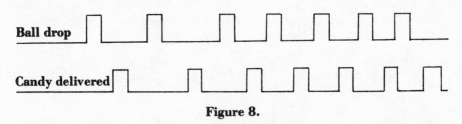

Figure 8.

3. The *consequence followed the behavior immediately*. There was little lag between the ball-dropping behavior and the delivery of the candy.
If the child were brought into the lab each day for a set period, seated in front of the box, and allowed to drop the ball and receive candy when he did, the ball would be dropped more and more, up to some limit. The limit, of course, depends on how rapidly this ball falls through the apparatus, how fast the child can pick up the ball and put it in the upper hole, and the amount of time the child

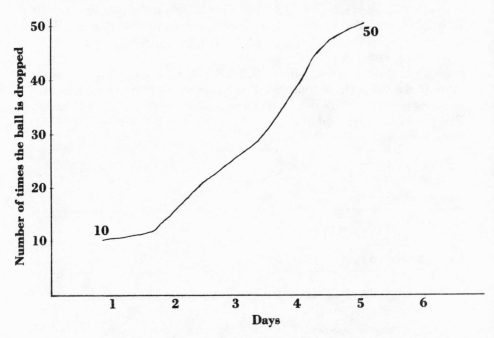

Figure 9. Frequency of ball droppings per day.

has in the room. The frequency of this behavior could be plotted as shown in Figure 9. This graph indicates that on the first day the child dropped the ball slightly less than ten times; on the second day, somewhat more, and then on each subsequent day there was an increase until the child was dropping the ball approximately fifty times a day (his limit). The graph shows there was an increase in the frequency of the behavior of concern: dropping the ball in the upper hole in the apparatus.

This same procedure—giving a child candy, food, or a toy immediately following the desired behavior—has been used in a variety of other situations. We had an opportunity to work with a young retarded girl who had not learned how to pay attention. "To pay attention" was defined behaviorally as her looking at the therapist's mouth or face when her name was called. The desired behavior was for her to fixate for a five-second period. To achieve this, the therapist placed his face close to hers and then called her name. She had little recourse other than to fixate on his face because of his closeness. When she did this for a five-second period, an M&M was placed in her mouth. Thus, the desired behavior was immediately followed by a piece of candy. This resulted in an increased frequency in attention-paying behavior, which, of course, is a prerequisite for any learning. We have also toilet-trained children, using positive reinforcement. This study will be presented in more detail later, but for now suffice it to say that the behavior (urinating in the toilet) was followed by giving the child an after-dinner mint.

TANGIBLE REINFORCERS

There are different kinds of reinforcers that can be used, but such reinforcers as candy, toys, and food are referred to as tangible reinforcers. Sometimes parents and others have been concerned about giving things to children for showing good behavior. It is somewhat difficult to understand such opposition. Certainly most parents give such things as toys, candy and cake to their children, although there have been cases in which the parents have withheld sweets from children because of the possible deleterious effect on their teeth. The opposition seems to take the view that children should not be rewarded for doing what they should be doing anyway. Those parents not infrequently use the word "bribe" for positive reinforcement procedures. Bribery is a loaded word and not really appropriate if one looks closely at its actual definition. Bribe is defined by the dictionary in different ways but it means to pervert one's judgment or to corrupt one's morals. Such words as "pervert" or "corrupt" are not appropriate when one is talking about teaching a retarded girl to pay attention or to help a child become toilet-trained. One point behaviorists make regarding the bribery issue is that, while it may seem crass, much adult behavior is followed by some tangible reinforcer. It is a rare person who would continue his job very long if no salary were forthcoming. Perhaps some of the concern might be that once a person receives a tangible reinforcement to help him learn a particular behavior, he will never in the future perform that behavior unless he is reinforced. If such were the case, obviously positive reinforcement would be a poor technique. Behaviorists do want to stop using tangible reinforcers as soon as possible. They do know, however, that in many situations the fastest and most efficient way to get the child to change his behavior is by using tangible positive reinforcers. Once that behavior is established, there are other procedures, to be discussed later, which will cover maintenance of a behavior, i.e., the child continues to perform on his own.

In looking at reinforcers more closely, there are several ways they may be categorized. The one type of reinforcer already discussed and, perhaps, the easiest to understand is the tangible reinforcer. There are three other kinds that should be mentioned: verbal reinforcers, token reinforcers, and attention as a reinforcer.

VERBAL REINFORCERS

Verbal reinforcers are relatively easy to see and understand. Certainly, saying "good boy" or "good girl" to a child when he or she has performed some task is a reinforcer. Parents know that when they have said such phrases they can almost see the child beam with pride. Such parents may also have noticed, if they kept records or observed closely, that the child will show an increase in behavior that is verbally reinforced.

TOKEN REINFORCERS

A token reinforcement is a symbol or token that can be used to obtain another reward, frequently a tangible one. Money is a good example of this kind of reinforcement. Money by itself has no value unless it can be spent for other things. With children, a variety of token situations have been devised. There was one situation in which a mother could not get her eight-year-old daughter to make her bed in the morning. The mother was a widow and had to work full time. The morning interaction between the mother and daughter was mainly yelling, nagging, and crying. It was not pleasant for either and the daughter frequently had to leave for school before she made her bed. The mother had had some exposure to the behavioral approach to rearing children and she decided to try it.

The mother had her daughter help her make a calendar with enough space on each day to affix a small bird seal. The bird seals had been selected by the child when she and her mother had gone shopping. The mother posted the calendar in the child's room and told her that each day she made her bed she would be allowed to paste a bird seal on that day on the calendar. The mother also said that if during that first week she had three bird seals pasted on, she would have a special surprise the following Saturday. The special surprise might be some candy, a trip to the zoo, or a toy. When the child earned three bird seals the first week, she was given some candy she especially liked. The second week, she was required to have four bird seals on her calendar to receive the surprise. This procedure of increasing the number of seals necessary to receive the surprise was continued until she made her bed every morning.

After six weeks, the child was making her bed regularly without any of the yelling or nagging that had gone on before. The bird seals were token reinforcements. The bird seals had value because they could be cashed in for the Saturday surprise. Other psychologists have used various pencil marks, given by a teacher or a parent, as token reinforcements. The point is that a certain number of pencil marks can be converted to some tangible reinforcement. We have worked with nursery-school children to teach them the names of colors.

Nursery-school teachers frequently use the names of colors as a beginning example of how word symbols are related to objects and events and, hence, the importance of having the child learn the names of colors. Originally, small trinkets, such as are found in penny gumball machines, were given for each correct response. It was soon discovered that the child was earning a great many trinkets, but because there were so many, the child was distracted from the task at hand. Using a procedure similar to that devised by others, a three- by five-inch card was divided into fifteen squares and a mark was made for each correct response. When a card was completed, the child was given the card and would receive one trinket. This worked much better. The child received fewer trinkets and the distraction was minimal.

ATTENTION AS A REINFORCER

A third type of reinforcer is simply paying attention to the child or turning the face toward the child and looking at him or her. If an adult pays attention immediately after some behavior of the child, there is apt to be an increase in the frequency of that behavior. The reinforcement value of paying attention may explain why children persist in some undesirable behavior when the parents feel they are punishing the child for this behavior. Thus, a child may misbehave, the parent then scolds or spanks the child, and still there is no reduction in the undesirable behavior. When this occurs, it is usually frustrating and perplexing to the parent. It is similar to the classroom situation when the unruly child is taking all of the teacher's time and yet the deviant behavior continues. On close analysis, it is seen that the child's disruptive behavior is followed by the teacher paying attention if only by scolding or by threatening to send the child to the principal's office.

WHY ARE CERTAIN REINFORCERS EFFECTIVE?

Why, one might ask, are verbal and token reinforcers, and paying attention reinforcing to a child? Perhaps this can best be explained by going back to the apparatus previously discussed—the box with two holes in it, one above the other. The child would place a ball in the top hole and a piece of candy would drop into the dish at the side. If this apparatus were changed slightly so that there was a small light placed above the dish where the candy fell (see Figure 10), when the ball is dropped in the top, this light flashes on for a brief period. The flash of the light is followed by the delivery of the candy and the ball then returns to the bottom hole. This can be diagrammed using an event recorder as indicated in Figure 11.

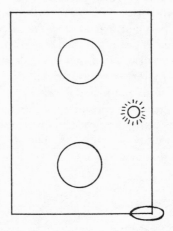

Figure 10. Apparatus to demonstrate conditioned reinforcement.

Assume that a child played with this apparatus, dropping the ball, seeing the light flash, and receiving candy, in that order. After this had taken place a number of times, one would discover that the child would continue to drop the ball, even though candy was not delivered, if the light lit each time he dropped the ball. The light is then said to be a conditioned reinforcer. Before the pairing began, the light was neutral as a reinforcer and, consequently, ineffective. After it was paired with the candy, it now became effective and is said to be conditioned. Even so, if the light were used alone, its effectiveness as a reinforcer

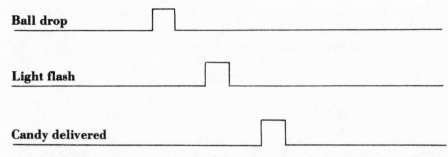

Figure 11. Event recorder diagram of conditioned reinforcement.

would wear out in time. The effectiveness of the light can be maintained, however, if every so often it is followed by the candy.

The reason verbal and token reinforcers and attention are effective is that they become conditioners in a manner similar to the light. Take a very early situation in an infant's life, when he is being fed by bottle. A mother frequently will take the baby in her arms, look at his face (so she can see where to put the nipple) and perhaps make cooing sounds or baby talk, and then put the nipple in the child's mouth. Notice that preceding the tangible reinforcement, milk, the mother has looked at the child (i.e., paid attention) and made noises. In infancy this pairing takes place around six to eight times a day. At a later age the child might say to his mother, "Mom, may I have a cookie?" She then turns her head and looks at him and says, "Yes, help yourself." The child then gets a cookie. Again, the attention paid by the mother is followed by her talking which, in turn, is followed by the cookie (i.e., tangible reinforcement). Even at a much later period, this sequence takes place. The child may say to his teacher, "May I get a drink of water?" The teacher looks at him and says, "Yes, you may," and the child then gets a drink. In each of these situations described, behavior could be plotted as was done with the ball-dropping apparatus. (See Figure 12.) The tangible reinforcement must follow the "paying attention" or "talking to" every so often, or the behavior will stop taking place.

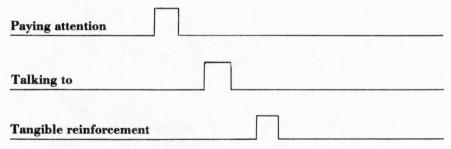

Figure 12. Event recorder diagram of conditioned reinforcement.

To review, then, there are four different kinds of reinforcements: tangible, verbal, token, and paying attention. A general rule seems to be that tangible reinforcers establish a new behavior more rapidly than the other reinforcements.

SATIATION-DEPRIVATION

It is important to be aware of a dimension of positive reinforcement alluded to earlier. To make the reinforcement effective, it must be something that the child desires and also something the child lacks. In studies done with children being toilet-trained using candy as a reinforcer, all other sources of candy were removed. The parents stopped buying candy and the candy dish was removed. Obviously, if the child has all the candy he wants at his disposal, he is said to be satiated, and offering candy to perform certain behaviors will not be effective. The concept of satiation-deprivation is important. If the ball-dropping apparatus mentioned earlier had delivered a hundred pieces of candy instead of one, the child would see that he had all the candy he could eat and probably would stop dropping the ball. The rule is that the reinforcements always be given in small amounts so that the child will continue to perform the desired behavior.

EFFORT REQUIRED IN REINFORCEMENT

It might be said that reinforcing particular behaviors of a child requires a great deal of effort. That is true, but one should remember that reinforcements are given to a child all the time. Parents frequently give children snacks, smiles, pats, kisses, trips to the zoo, and movies. These are reinforcing the behavior that precedes them and are given in a random manner. Perhaps parents are reinforcing the very behavior they feel is undesirable.

NEGATIVE REINFORCEMENT

While positive reinforcement is the most effective way of increasing the frequency of behaviors, there is another procedure called negative reinforcement. Negative reinforcement is used less but it is important to know about because it helps explain behavior that, at first, might seem puzzling. Negative reinforcement is probably more difficult to understand than positive reinforcement. It refers to the behavior that is associated with the conclusion of some aversive situation. A large dog chasing a child is viewed by that child as aversive and the child will try to "turn off" that situation as soon as he can by running into the house, climbing a tree, or calling for help. Suppose he escapes the dog by running into the house, then, when confronted by a vicious dog again, he will run into the house. If this situation occurs routinely, he will run into the house more and more frequently, or there will be an increase in the frequency of the behavior in question. This situation with the dog might be diagrammed with an event recorder as presented in Figure 13. In Figure 13 it is noted that the child tried several behaviors (A, B, C) but they were not associated with removing the dog. Running into the house was, however.

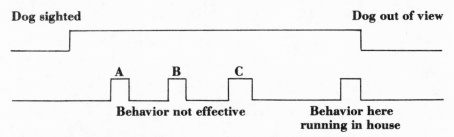

Figure 13. Diagram of negative reinforcement.

ESCAPE LEARNING

A more complex example explaining other aspects of negative reinforcement is that of a mother spanking a child. Assume the mother discovers the child has done something wrong. She wants to punish him and calls him into the house, telling him he is going to get a spanking. The mother then starts spanking him (the aversive stimulus). The child searches through his behaviors in an attempt to stop the spanking. He may tell his mother he hates her, he may kick and hit, or he may start crying. Let us assume that when he tells his mother he hates her, she continues spanking. The child then will try kicking and hitting. This, too, has no effect on the spanking. He then starts crying. The mother may say to herself, "Well, I finally got through to him" and stops spanking. This could be diagrammed as presented in Figure 14.

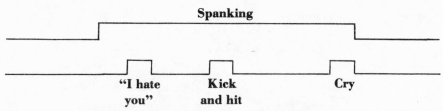

Figure 14. Diagram of negative reinforcement.

The crying is associated with the termination of the aversive stimulus—the spanking. Let us assume that the boy frequently displays behavior his mother considers undesirable. The next day he again performs some undesirable behavior and again his mother calls him in for his daily spanking. This time when she starts spanking, she will find that she is able to get through to him sooner than before: He starts crying earlier. Or stated another way, the behaviors that he tried before (saying, "I hate you" or kicking and hitting) were not effective and were not subsequently used. A diagram to illustrate this is presented in Figure 15.

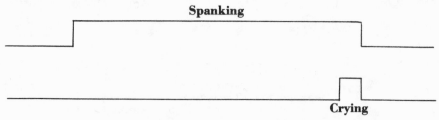

Figure 15. Diagram of negative reinforcement.

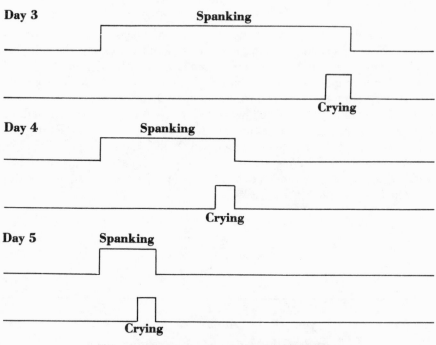

Figure 16. Example of escape learning.

Crying is associated with the termination of the spanking, so it is likely to be repeated more frequently. As this daily spanking continues, and the mother and child perform consistently, the spanking will take less and less time as indicated in Figure 16. This has been termed escape learning, as the child has learned to escape the spanking, although some spanking still does take place.

AVOIDANCE LEARNING

To return to the spanking example, remember that the mother called the child and told him he was going to get a spanking. The diagram used before could be modified to include that calling as shown in Figure 17.

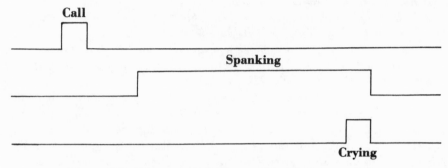

Figure 17. Diagram of mother calling before spanking.

If the mother continues her daily spankings (and callings), she will discover that the child will start crying sooner and sooner after the spanking starts. If the routine continues, she will notice another change. Eventually when she calls the

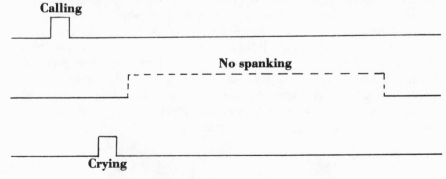

Figure 18. Example of avoidance learning.

child, he will start crying even before the spanking has begun. If the mother says to herself, "Well, he obviously is sorry for what he has done and so I'll not spank him," she can be sure that when she says, "Come in for your spanking," he will start crying. If diagrammed this event would be shown in Figure 18. The spanking record is a dotted line to show that when the child starts crying, soon the spanking will not take place. The situation in which the child does not receive a spanking, because he cries after he is called, is avoidance learning.

There are many examples of negative reinforcement that take place in everyday situations. Analyze the following situations:

1. *Jimmy is in the third grade. There is an older boy in the fifth grade who threatens him and sometimes hits him. Jimmy has to go home the same way as the older boy and has often been chased by him. Jimmy's mother has noticed that Jimmy almost always comes home breathless from running.*

2. *Mary has never done very well in school, although her work has not been very far below average. Over the last year, whenever a test is scheduled, Mary develops a headache or stomachache and stays home. Her mother has always been concerned about Mary's health, but the doctor can find nothing wrong. Mary is staying home sick more and more.*

3. *Bill is fourteen and while he has gotten along well with his parents in the past, he has had more problems recently. What starts out as an innocent comment leads to a discussion, which leads to an argument. Bill feels he is criticized for his views, his way of dress, his work at school, and he feels his parents do not understand him. Over the last two months, as soon as such a discussion starts, he leaves the house. He has been spending less and less time at home and his parents are concerned.*

SUMMARY

Techniques for increasing frequencies of behavior were discussed. The concept of positive reinforcement, in which the behavior of concern is followed by some consequence over a period of time resulting in an increase in frequency of behavior, was introduced. Various types of reinforcers were discussed: tangible reinforcers, verbal reinforcers, token reinforcers, and attention. The importance of satiation and deprivation for positive reinforcement was pointed out. The concept of negative reinforcement occurs in situations involving behavior that is associated with the ending of some aversive situation. Escape and avoidance learning involve this kind of reinforcement.

Chapter 4

Reducing the Frequency of Behaviors

Parents have a tendency to become much more upset about undesirable behaviors of their children than they do about desirable behaviors their children fail to exhibit. One reason is that if a child does not display certain behaviors the parents feel are important, they can hope that such behavior will eventually emerge. The undesirable behavior, however, is here today, right now, and can be most irksome. The particularly undesirable behavior may also be frowned upon by society, and a child enacting such behavior tells the world that somehow his or her parents were deficient. Thus, if a child wets his pants, picks his nose, says a dirty word, or uses bad table manners, the parents may feel that they have erred in raising the child. Some examples are:

1. Jerry is four years old and he and his mother have been working on his toilet-training problem for some time. She has been punitive on occasions and, at other times, very permissive. Jerry, on the other hand, has used the toilet appropriately for a period and then has slipped. Lately, she has discovered that he has had his bowel movement almost any place but the toilet, e.g., in his closet, outdoors, and in the basement.

2. Kathy is eleven and involved in several activities connected with church and school. Sometimes she goes directly to her girl friend's house and does not tell her parents. When she does not come home, they become upset and try to find her. They have impressed upon her that she should let them

29

know when she is coming home and where she will be, but she still forgets occasionally. On one occasion the police were called.

3. Frank is fourteen. His parents were shocked when the police brought him home one day and told them Frank had been caught shoplifting candy at a nearby drugstore.

4. Betty, who is three and a half, spends a great deal of her time whining and crying. This behavior subsides at times but, especially if she is tired or wants something, she becomes loud and upsets her mother.

In each of the above cases, certain behavior takes place that the parents would like to reduce or eliminate. If a record were kept of the above behaviors and plotted, it would appear as shown in Figure 19. What is desired, of course, is to have the behavior reduced in frequency so it appears as shown in Figure 20.

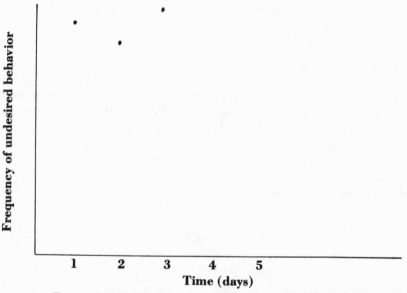

Figure 19. Example of undesired behavior charted.

This chapter will present some of the behavioral methods designed to reduce frequencies of behavior. Before going into these, however, it is necessary to digress somewhat and discuss two different kinds of learning.

BEHAVIOR TO CHANGE THE ENVIRONMENT—OPERANT BEHAVIOR

The first kind of learning is the one that has already been discussed. It is the learning involved when a child is trying to change whatever is happening to him

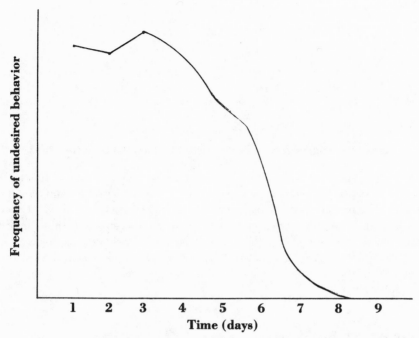

Figure 20. Example of undesired behavior reduced to zero.

or to change his environment. A hungry baby will cry, and his mother will bring a bottle of milk. The child's behavior (crying) is an attempt to change his environment (to have someone bring a bottle). The older child who wants a cookie will go to the cookie jar and take one. He has changed his environment (placed himself close to the cookie jar) by his behavior (walking to the kitchen and approaching the cookie jar). The child who wants attention from his mother may pinch his baby brother. His mother then talks to him or yells at him and asks him why he hurt his baby brother. He changed his environment (his mother paid attention to him) following his behavior of pinching his brother.

Many other obvious examples come to mind; you should watch your own children or others to observe the behavior that takes place to change the environment. While in the examples cited above, each behavior was effective in changing the child's environment, frequently behaviors designed to change the environment are not effective. If, after frequently repeating one behavior, the environment in question does not change, the child will switch to another behavior. If this second behavior proves ineffective, it too will stop and another behavior will take its place. This will continue until a behavior works (i.e., one associated with a change in environment) or the child gives up. One might diagram such a sequence as presented in Figure 21.

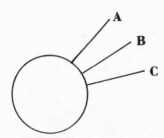

Figure 21. Diagram of different behaviors available to the child.

If A, B, and C are viewed as different behaviors, the child would first try A. He would repeat behavior A until he found it ineffective, give up and switch to B. If that too proved ineffective, then he would move on to behavior C. If C were effective in changing the environment, C would become stronger while A and B would become weaker and, in the future, behavior C would be most likely to occur. This kind of learning is called operant because it operates on the environment. All of the examples presented in the book so far have been examples of operant learning.

Respondent Behavior

But there is another kind of learning that is important for understanding the behavior of children. Its importance lies in the fact that it is related to anxiety or fear. This learning is different from operant in several respects. Rather than behavior being emitted by the child, it is caused by some preceding stimulus. That is, the child's behavior follows the stimulus that elicits it, rather than the behavior coming first. This kind of behavior is called respondent behavior. The child will cry when his finger is stuck with a pin. A bright light in the child's eyes will bring about a contraction of his pupils. Again, the behavior follows the stimulus. Other examples: a speck in the eye, followed by watering of the eye; a tap on the patellar tendon, followed by a kicking out of the leg. Much of this is more physiological than operant behavior.

Fear and Anxiety

Respondent behavior is, for the most part, less important than operant behavior in everyday life, but it does help to explain fear and anxiety. A loud noise will elicit a certain kind of behavior in anyone, adult or child. A person will extend his arms, flex his knees, open his eyes wide, and a variety of physiological changes will take place: breathing will change, the person may perspire, the heartbeat will speed up, his stomach will contract, and so forth. Any of a child's frightening experiences will cause these particular internal changes to take place. When such an experience does take place, the child is said to be afraid, scared, upset, and he or she will frequently show other behaviors, such as sobbing, crying, or screaming.

Parents, of course, try to see that their child avoids as many of these frightening experiences as possible. As the child grows older, certain events take place, however, that place him in an upsetting situation. Some of these events are known to parents and attempts are made to minimize their impact, while other events occur that are not viewed as frightening by the parents and they are surprised when the child becomes upset. Almost all parents are aware that the various immunization shots and vaccinations hurt and are frightening to the child. For some children getting a haircut, sitting on a department-store Santa Claus's lap, going to school, can also be frightening. A disadvantage of having a child experience such a frightening event is that once he has experienced it, if he is again placed in such a situation in the future, he will become frightened again. The example of a child being afraid of a doctor because of having had some immunization shot can be shown in Figure 22.

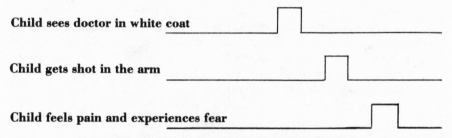

Child sees doctor in white coat

Child gets shot in the arm

Child feels pain and experiences fear

Figure 22. Example of conditioned fear.

Notice the respondent behavior when the child receives the shot in the arm. The various physiological changes called fear are elicited. If the pain is sufficiently intense, the sight of the doctor is said to be a conditioned stimulus. Parents who have had such a problem with a child will know how upset a child can get at the mere prospect of going to the doctor. It is as if just mentioning going to the doctor elicits the fear responses that were originally brought about by being stuck by the needle. The child may exhibit this same response when confronted with anyone in a white coat and, indeed, this sometimes is an explanation for a child's reluctance to get into a barber's chair.

A similar analysis can be made of many situations in which children show fear. We are familiar with a case (which will be presented in more detail in Chapter Eleven) in which toilet-training was the problem. Little success was achieved until it was discovered that the child, when about two, had been in the bathroom at a time when the toilet overflowed. There was much excitement and yelling by the parents and the child had become quite frightened. Each time in the future when placed on the toilet, the child showed fear or respondent behavior. Consequently, toilet-training did not progress well at all.

INTERACTION OF RESPONDENT AND OPERANT BEHAVIOR

While respondent and operant behaviors have been discussed separately, it should be pointed out that frequently both take place at the same time. In the example cited earlier about the child receiving the immunization shots, the respondent behavior (fear) was mentioned. Anyone familiar with such a situation is aware that there is also operant behavior. The child will try not to go to the doctor's office and if taken there, will try to avoid going into the doctor's office. He is thus trying to change the environment so that the doctor and the doctor's office are not visible to him. It should also be pointed out that behavior that may have a strong respondent component with a small amount of operant behavior may change over time to just the opposite. Take a hungry infant who shows respondent behavior by crying because of the pain he or she is experiencing. When he does cry, his mother comes to him and thus reinforces this crying behavior. If this takes place frequently, it is likely that at times, when the child is experiencing no pain (i.e., no hunger, cold, wetness), he will attempt to get his mother's attention by crying. He thus will attempt to change his environment by bringing his mother into view. More than likely he will be successful; mothers usually respond when their children cry.

At some point, however, the mother will say to herself, "That is not respondent crying; that is operant crying." She will probably not say it in those words. More likely she will say something like, "There's nothing wrong with him; he just wants me to pick him up." In the same way that there is a reduction in the respondent aspect of a behavior and an increase in the operant component over time, the above example of the doctor's immunization can be analyzed. While the child is frightened at first and shows respondent behavior, if he is successful in avoiding future visits to the doctor's office (i.e., if his mother says something like "He's too upset to take him to the doctor today, let's wait until next week,") the behavior will become more and more operant-oriented because it has successfully changed the environment.

PUNISHMENT

To return to the original intent of the chapter—how to decrease undesirable behaviors—the technique that probably stands out because of its popularity is punishment. Punishment, as used in everyday language, encompasses a wide variety of techniques. Perhaps it would be wise to define punishment in a precise behavioral way: Punishment is said to take place when some aversive stimulus

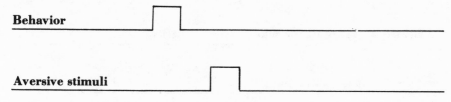

Figure 23. Diagram of punishment.

follows a behavior and there is a subsequent decrease in the frequency of that behavior. This is diagrammed in Figure 23. Thus, the child reaches out to stick his finger in the newly frosted cake and his mother slaps his hand. The behavior (reaching) is followed by an aversive stimulus (the slap). Notice the behavior and the aversive stimulus in the following examples:

1. *Kenneth was three years old when he was playing in the kitchen one day. His mother was baking and he accidentally touched the hot oven. He was not burned badly, but his hand did become red and inflamed, and he cried. Since then, he has avoided the kitchen somewhat and the oven in particular. His mother said that he learned his lesson and that "the burnt child fears the flame."*

2. *Sherry had just turned three in the spring. All winter long, she had been cooped up in the house; when the weather did turn nice, her mother allowed her to play outside. When her mother's back was turned, Sherry ran into the street after a dog. Her mother, frightened because Sherry ran into the busy street, spanked Sherry quite severely. Sherry does not go into the street any more.*

3. *Jack is six and heard some older boys using dirty words. When he came home, he repeated them to his mother who became quite upset and washed his mouth out with a strong-tasting soap.*

In each of these examples, the behavior is followed by an aversive stimulus. To a certain extent punishment defined in this manner is analogous to positive reinforcement, except the behavior decreases in frequency rather than increases. Now punishment, in a manner similar to positive reinforcement, can be associated with other stimuli so that those stimuli work as effectively as the original stimulus. In the example above, in which the child is reaching to take some frosting from the cake, assume that mother said, "No" as she slapped his hand.

If she paired the saying of no a sufficient number of times with the slap, the child would eventually respond as if the no were the slap. It is diagrammed in Figure 24. In time, the saying of no would serve as the punishment and the behavior would cease when the mother said no. It is shown in Figure 25.

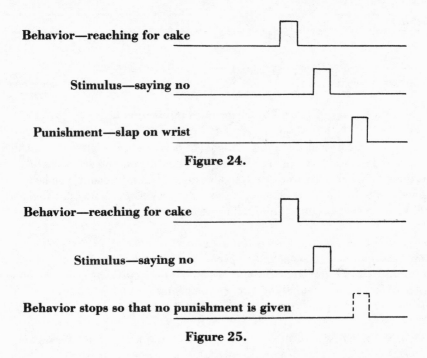

Figure 24.

Figure 25.

In observing the child in this circumstance, one would notice that he behaves about the same whether the mother slaps his hand or not. Initially, the child would stop reaching for the cake when his hand is slapped. He might withdraw his hand rapidly and put it behind him or he might start to cry. If closer internal observation were available, it would show that his heart started to beat faster, his stomach contracted, and his breathing rate changed. At a later time, when he started to reach for the cake and his mother said no, the same behaviors would take place, i.e., the rapid withdrawal of the hand, then crying, and the physiological changes. Over the years, the mother may add another cue, such as frowning, so that the sequence of punishment for a child would consist of the undesired behavior, followed by the frown, followed by the no, followed by the slap. If this takes place, it is eventually possible for the mother to stop some behavior of the child by a frown. The child will react as if he or she had been slapped on the wrist. Other parents may use a particular tone of voice before they say "No," which is followed by the slap. If so, then the child's behavior will cease as soon as the child hears the parent use that tone of voice. A mother can then control her child's behavior by a frown or by saying "No" or "Stop that."

While punishment as described above seems relatively simple, a closer behavioral analysis will show that it is actually complex. Its complexity is revealed when the different components are analyzed. First, there needs to be positive reinforcement for the undesirable behavior to take place initially. Looking at the plotting of behavior frequency, there must be something maintaining the behavior.

In the situation with the boy reaching for the cake, he had been reinforced in the past by eating the frosting. The undesirable behavior would probably not have taken place had the mother placed a bowl of mashed potatoes on the table. The second factor involved is the respondent behavior. The slap on the wrist brings about physiological changes as well as the crying. Finally, negative reinforcement is involved. Remember that with behavior associated with the termination of an aversive stimulus, there will be an increase in the frequency of that behavior. In the cake-frosting example, the boy might withdraw his hand rapidly and put it behind his back as far as possible from the mother's slapping hand. If there has been enough wrist slapping, the child may frequently place his hand behind his back as he approaches no-no situations. This explains, in a more precise manner, the effectiveness of punishment in eliminating a behavior. Obviously, if the child goes around with his hand behind his back (because of negative reinforcement), he cannot exhibit the undesirable behavior of reaching for the cake's frosting. The undesirable behavior is eliminated because of negative reinforcement, not because of punishment.

EXERCISES—PUNISHMENT

Analyze behaviorally the following situations:

1. *Lisa, who is three, has never had any pets of her own. One day her mother took her to visit a friend and while her mother and friend were talking, Lisa began playing with the friend's cat. As Lisa had had little experience with pets, she pulled the cat's tail. The cat, in turn, clawed Lisa's hand and Lisa ran crying to her mother. Her mother now notices that Lisa runs to her at the sight of any cat.*

2. *Mary is five and quite active. One day she played in the mud and when she came home, her mother was very upset because she had soiled her clothes. She started to spank Mary and Mary said that her mother didn't love her. Her mother calmed down somewhat at this, stopped spanking Mary and told her she did love her but that she did get angry about Mary getting so dirty. She has noticed that on other occasions Mary is now saying that her mother doesn't love her.*

3. *Eight-year-old Jerry is in the third grade. He is quite concerned about doing well in school and when the class misbehaved and the teacher scolded the whole class, he started to cry. The teacher stopped scolding them, took Jerry to one side, and told him to stop crying. It seems that the teacher has noticed Jerry crying more now than before.*

ADVANTAGES AND DISADVANTAGES OF PUNISHMENT

The use of punishment to reduce the frequency of undesirable behaviors seems to have more disadvantages than advantages. One prominent advantage is that when punishment is used, the behavior usually ceases rapidly. There is no gradual reduction in the frequency of the behavior; the behavior usually stops

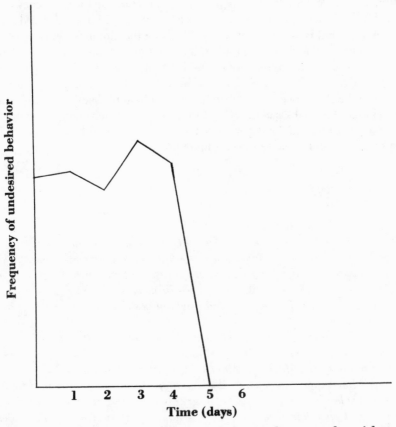

Figure 26. Diagram of rapid change in behavior because of punishment.

immediately. It is plotted in Figure 26. Punishment's advantage, of course, is that a parent can decide whether he or she wants an abrupt cessation of the behavior; if so, punishment is probably most effective. Any behavior placing a child in a potentially injurious position would be so considered. Thus, playing with electrical equipment, running into the street, or playing with fire are typical examples.

There are disadvantages, however, in using punishment that all parents should be aware of. One important consideration is the emotional aspect (respondent behavior), which has some negative effects. In any situation learned under emotional circumstances, it seems difficult to do any relearning. Consequently, as the child becomes older and needs to evaluate situations differently, he or she will find this difficult. Probably the greatest disadvantage of punishment is that the child learns to avoid the punisher, so the main thing a child will have learned is to stay away from his or her parents. Obviously, future communication will be greatly reduced and, if such a situation continues, there will be little interaction between the child and his parents. This, of course, is not good for future learning. The third problem with punishment is that it only tells the child what behavior not to display, it does not tell him what the desired behavior is. It seems that some children who have been punished frequently display few behaviors, i.e., they are greatly restricted in their behaviors and show less variety of expression.

One might ask: why do parents persist in punishment or why is punishment so popular if it has these bad effects? There are at least two answers. One is that parents are not aware of the negative effects cited above. Another reason is that the parent is reinforced for using punishment. The parent, in attempting to change his or her environment, will spank or hit a child. The annoying behavior of the child immediately ceases and the parent is reinforced for his or her behavior.

EXTINCTION

Another procedure effective in reducing the frequency of behaviors is extinction. Extinction removes the reinforcement that is maintaining the behavior. In the example cited under positive reinforcement (in which the box with two holes was used), extinction would take place if the candy stopped falling into the tray. Thus, the child who had been dropping the ball frequently, receiving candy each time, would stop responding if candy was no longer forthcoming. The same effect can be achieved in other situations by first finding out what the reinforcement is and then removing it.

In the situations where candy is used, it is easy to see the reinforcement but the difficulty arises when attention serves as a reinforcer. Parents very frequently can eliminate an undesirable behavior by simply ignoring it. The child-rearing books and child experts have not really emphasized the value of extinction in changing behavior. Perhaps one of the reasons is that records of the frequency of a behavior have not usually been kept. If this is not done, extinction seems to be a slow process, so slow that at times nothing seems to be happening.

There are probably changes in the behavior of children that should be attributed to extinction but are not. One hypothetical case: A preschooler had been displaying temper-tantrum behavior more and more frequently. The mother, in desperation, says that she can take no more and consults a child expert. The child expert asks the mother how old the child is and, hearing that he is two and one-half, tells her that many children of this age show temper tantrums. The therapist might go on to state that, since this is a developmental phase, the child will outgrow it. The mother, relieved that the problem is not serious, is not so upset and shows less concern about the child's tantrums. The child will throw his tantrums in an attempt to control his mother, but she no longer reinforces the behavior by paying attention. Eventually, through extinction, the tantrums will diminish and then cease. The mother will report that the difficulty was correctly diagnosed and the child did indeed outgrow the phase. More precisely, however, the mother used extinction, which was responsible for reducing frequency of the tantrum behavior.

TIME-OUT PROCEDURES

The third and last method is sometimes confused with both of the other two. It consists of the removing of positive reinforcement following the behavior. The positive reinforcement is not, however, the positive reinforcement that is maintaining the behavior. An example will clarify the definition. If a child is watching a TV show at the same time he pokes his little sister, his mother might say, "You hit her one more time and I'm going to turn off the TV." The mother hopes for a reduction in poking behavior. If his behavior does persist, she will turn off the TV. This might be diagrammed as shown in Figure 27.

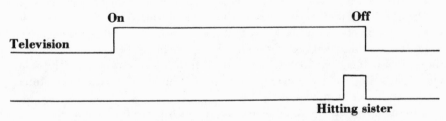

Figure 27. Example of removal of positive reinforcement.

The poking behavior now becomes associated with the TV's removal. Remember that the operating TV was not responsible for maintaining the poking behavior. The reinforcement for the poking behavior may have been the reinforcement he got from his sister's behavior or the attention from his mother. Another familiar example: Assume a child had shown some undesirable behavior and was forced to stand in the corner. The positive reinforcement removed here, however, is less clear than the TV. In this situation, the positive reinforcement has several different aspects that are available to the child when he is not restricted to the corner. Thus he could run, look at TV, play with various toys, talk to others, and so forth. By being placed in the corner, all of these are, in effect, removed from him. This technique of removing positive reinforcement from the child to reduce undesirable behavior is called a *time-out procedure*. Notice that it differs from extinction because with extinction, the reinforcement that maintains the behavior is removed, while in the time-out procedure, removing the positive reinforcement does not maintain the behavior. Some individuals have called the time-out procedure punishment, e.g., the child is sent to his room as a punishment. It seems worthwhile, in our experience, to keep the two separate for at least two reasons. One is that time-out is a much more neutral word than punishment. There are many connotations of the word "punishment" that do not help a person think clearly about what is taking place. The second reason for viewing them separately is that there usually is a lot less emotion or respondent behavior on the child's part associated with time-out than there is with punishment.

SUMMARY

In this chapter three procedures for reducing the frequency of behavior have been presented. Punishment, following the undesired behavior by an aversive stimulus, is one. There are, however, certain disadvantages to using punishment. One is that there is the emotional or respondent component involved in punishment. Second, and probably the most important, is that the child learns to avoid the punisher. Third, in using punishment the child is not told what behavior is desired, only that certain behavior is inappropriate.

The second procedure was extinction in which the stimulus reinforcing the behavior is removed. The last procedure, time-out, involved the removal of positive reinforcement following the undesired behavior.

Chapter 5

Increasing and
Decreasing Behaviors

The techniques mentioned so far have been concerned with increasing or decreasing behaviors. For learning purposes, it is best to view them initially in
this way. However, when actually dealing with a problem, a parent should use a
double-barreled approach: a reduction of the undesirable behavior and an increase of a desirable behavior that is incompatible with the undesired behavior.
One example we use can be applied to thumb-sucking. The parent is, of course,
concerned with the child's ceasing this undesirable behavior. A variety of techniques may be used. The parents can stop paying attention to the child's thumb-
sucking; thus, any reinforcement the child was receiving from the parents' attention for thumb-sucking is removed. This may have some effect although it is
doubtful because the child receives some conditioned reinforcement from
thumb-sucking. The parent may punish the child so that each time the child puts
his thumb in his mouth he or she will be slapped. Thus, each time the undesirable behavior occurs, it is followed by an aversive stimulus.

A very different way of viewing the problem would be to think of a desirable behavior that is incompatible with thumb-sucking. The example we use is
to teach the child to put his thumb in his ear. If his thumb is in his ear, it cannot
be in his mouth. Getting the incompatible behavior (thumb in the ear) to take
place can be achieved by using the techniques cited in this chapter. In this manner the parent could approach the problem of thumb-sucking, and solve it, by
reinforcing the child for keeping his thumb in his ear. Parents would no longer

be troubled with thumb-sucking, as it has been behaviorally defined, if the child kept his thumb in his ear. They may now, however, be confronted by another undesirable behavior (i.e., thumb in the ear), but that too is soluble by behavioral techniques so that eventually his thumb would be kept in a normal position.

Looking for an incompatible but desirable behavior is somewhat difficult to understand and implement at first. Probably the main reason for the almost exclusive focus on the undesirable behavior is that it commands the attention of parents. The problem does not show itself until the undesirable behavior takes place. Then there is frequently shouting, punishing, or comments to the spouse such as, "We must do something about that boy." If the undesirable behavior does not take place, the family functions relatively smoothly and the behavior is not thought of by either the parents or child.

Another example frequently displayed by teachers in one way or another involved disruptive children. The teacher might say to a boy who is hitting his companion and being inattentive, "Paul, you come up here and help me erase the board." Paul will then go to the front of the room, erase the board, and be thanked by the teacher. While he is erasing the board, it is obvious that he cannot be disruptive at the back of the class. The teacher's reinforcement of his effort in erasing the board is an example of the teacher reinforcing desirable behavior (erasing the board) that is incompatible with being disruptive in the back of the class (the undesired behavior). The teacher must be alert that he or she does not reinforce a chain of behaviors (disruption leading to erasing of board leading to reinforcement) or there will be an increase in disruptive behavior. One of the ways she might do this is to occasionally ask Paul to help her erase the board before he does something disruptive, therefore, giving him reinforcement (attention) for positive behavior. This may help to maintain the positive and minimize the disruptive behavior.

The example cited in the first chapter—of two children arguing or fighting—can be illustrative of this approach. The behavior the parents found undesirable was the arguing and fighting. The way to help these parents would, of course, first focus on reducing these behaviors by techniques previously mentioned. Viewing the problem in terms of incompatible behaviors, the parents should describe and define behaviors in which fighting does *not* take place while the children are together. One class of behaviors can be called cooperative. Any time the children are playing nicely together, helping each other with a task, sharing some of their toys or other property, the parents should reinforce that behavior. The reinforcements could be tangible ("You children have played so nicely together this afternoon, let's go out and get some ice cream."), or verbal ("Bobby, I like the way you shared your balloons with your sister."). If these parental reactions are reinforcing, there will be an increase in cooperative play and sharing. These behaviors, it is emphasized, are not compatible with hitting, fighting, and teasing.

For every undesirable behavior there is a desirable behavior that is incompatible. What would the desirable behaviors be that are incompatible with the following: (1) thumb-sucking; (2) teasing a sister; (3) whining to get a cookie; (4) talking loudly; (5) staying up late; (6) wetting one's pants; (7) not doing one's homework; (8) not eating vegetables?

As desirable incompatible behaviors increase, the frequency of undesirable behaviors decreases if only because less time is available for them.

COMMUNICATION OF RULES

It seems appropriate at this point to present something that has been alluded to earlier: clear communication of the rules children are to follow. Naturally with very young children this may present some difficulty, but as soon as the child is able to understand, spelling out the rules becomes important. Usually parents give little thought to the rules children should follow; they react only *after* the child has done something they disapprove of. Some parents, by making too many unclear rules, tend to defeat their own purpose. There are several factors that seem to be important as far as rules are concerned. Careful thought should be given as to whether such a rule is necessary; if it is possible to avoid making a rule, then do so.

The rule should be short and concise and care should be taken to make sure that both the parent and child agree on its meaning. It seems better to have the rule stated positively as if such behavior is expected. For example, "We will have dinner about six each evening," "You are expected to call if you are not coming directly home from school," and "You will practice your piano for one half hour each evening." Obviously compliance with the rules should be reinforced, at least every so often. The longer the child complies with the rules, the less need for reinforcement each time. If the child does not conform to the rules, it may be necessary to attach a second part to the rules. It may involve, preferably, something positive that will happen to him if he complies. That reinforcement should follow each time the child conforms to the rule. Thus, each time a child says "Excuse me" as he or she passes in front of a guest, the parent should point out how polite the child is. Although less strongly suggested, the parent can tie some undesirable consequence to breaking the rules. A child who does not appear in time for the evening meal does not eat. A further elaboration on rules will be presented when contracting is discussed.

It is important for parents to remember that once they have established consequences for complying with or breaking the rules, they should stick by them. If they find they are not, they should as quickly as possible revise the rules and discuss that change with the child. Only in this way can they expect the child to continue to comply with the set rules.

CONTRACTING

The position taken on rules is related to another technique for increasing or decreasing behavior. It is essentially withholding or withdrawing a positive reinforcement until a behavior is performed (desired behavior) or until it ceases to be performed (undesired behavior). This position is presented in an excellent book by Lloyd Homme, entitled *How to Use Contingency Contracting in the Classroom.* Thus a contract is made with a child stating that if he does something (or ceases doing something), then he can engage in some other activity that he finds reinforcing. The contract is clearly spelled out in detail in behavioral terms. An example would be that a child must put away the dishes and then he or she can watch a favorite TV show.

Think of some child with whom you are familiar. Then make two lists: one consisting of behaviors the child should do and the second, activities that the child likes to do. By looking over the list one might see how they can be paired in such a way that the task done is paired with a task that the child likes. In this manner, a child can be taught new things or perform tasks important for the operation of the home.

ARRANGING THE ENVIRONMENT

The third approach to increase or decrease behaviors changes the environment. It is obvious that by arranging the environment in a different way, certain behaviors are more or less likely to occur. An example we use in lectures concerns the problem that supermarkets have when customers take the shopping carts home with them or at least out of close range of the store. This is a costly problem for supermarkets and they have tried various methods to reduce this behavior. Care, of course, must be taken by the store manager not to offend customers. Some customers prefer to wheel the cart out to their car in the car lot. Then, rather than return the cart, they sometimes abandon it in the car lot. Sometimes people take the carts home for a variety of uses or individuals who do not have a car wheel their groceries all the way home.

One store we are familiar with coped with the problem by making it impossible to remove the carts from the store. The entrance to the store and the aisle through the check-out counter were too narrow for the carts to pass through. A conveyor belt was installed and a man on duty was present to place the groceries on the belt and another man to put the groceries into the customer's car. Thus, the undesirable behavior could not take place. An advantage of this approach is that the frustration is usually not directed at an individual as it would be if the manager stopped people from leaving the store with a cart. Frequently the response is an accepting one.

This same approach can and is being used in dealing with children. Most parents go through a period in which their child, usually around one or two, pulls magazines off the coffee table and other low places and throws them on the floor. If the problem is greater than average, it will be observed that the parents have arranged the environment so that there are few loose objects below about three feet from the floor. The parents coped with the problem by changing the environment—removing all objects the child can get into and placing them out of his reach. The particular problem has been solved.

Think of ways in which environmental change would solve these problems: (1) snacking between meals; (2) losing mittens; (3) watching too much TV; (4) hitting brother or sister.

INCREASING DESIRABLE BEHAVIORS

It should be emphasized that the preceding on effects of changing environments centered on reducing undesirable behaviors. The same approach, however, is and can be used to increase desirable behaviors. A laboratory situation can serve as an example. Suppose a child is placed in a room that is barren and devoid of anything. Then a single toy is placed in the room. The odds then are fairly high the child will play with that toy. Thus, by arranging the environment in a particular way (putting a toy in a barren room), we have brought about a particular behavior (playing with said toy). To carry this over to the home, it is obvious the child will not exhibit behaviors for which the environment has not been arranged. Stated another way, the child will not learn something that has not been present in his environment. A girl who has never seen a doll will not be adept at doll-playing. A boy who has never received a toy gun will know little about guns. The child who never handles any money will have more difficulty making change than a child who has had such experiences. The child who has many books available will more likely to read than the child who has few or none. One will notice that children frequently have the same interests as the parents. One of the reasons for this is that the environment is arranged in such a way that the child can learn and be exposed to particular events. Another reason, of course, is that the child is reinforced by parents for taking part in such activities.

Think how the environment could be arranged so that there would be a greater likelihood for the child to show the following behaviors: (1) a boy to build a bird house and other woodworking tasks; (2) a girl who likes to learn new words; (3) a child who is knowledgeable about electricity and likes to repair electrical appliances.

SUMMARY

This chapter has emphasized some of the more advanced techniques effective in both reducing or increasing the frequency of certain behaviors. It was pointed out that in dealing with a problem, several techniques should be used at the same time. Thus, one can use extinction of an undesirable behavior at the same time an incompatible behavior is being reinforced. The importance of communication and establishing rules with the child was stressed. Contracting was also presented as well as modification of the environment.

Chapter 6

Changing a Child's Behavior

This chapter will present several psychological concepts needed to round out the reader's knowledge of children from a behavioral viewpoint. The first area of concern is the initiation of desired behaviors and the second is how to

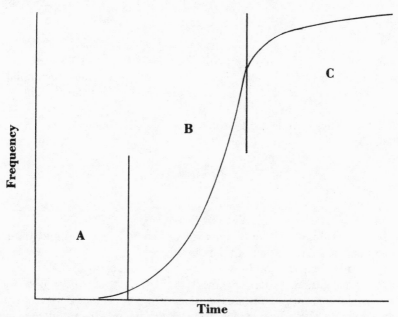

Figure 28. A curve showing increase in frequency of behavior (B), before behavior present (A), and after behavior has been learned well (C).

help the behavior take place for a long period of time without reinforcement every time. Stated another way, this chapter covers what occurs before and after a desired behavior is decreased in frequency or an undesired behavior is increased. So far this book has focused on how undesirable behaviors can be reduced or how desirable behaviors can be increased. A curve plotting an increase or decrease in behaviors is one way of viewing the material presented so far. (See Figure 28.) We might look at the curve in terms of three different parts. If we focus on the curve representing an increase in behaviors—the middle part of the curve, part B—we have discussed how behaviors that have a low frequency can be made to have a high frequency. Part A, in which the behavior does *not* take place at all, has not been discussed and yet is quite important. Obviously, if the behavior does not take place, a parent can stand and wait until the M & Ms melt in his hand. One of the aims of this chapter will be to discuss how the behavioral approach can help a child to learn a behavior he or she has never shown. The third part of the curve (part C) will also be discussed, a part about which parents are most concerned—when the child begins to display the desired behaviors with minimal or no parental involvement. The child is now taking out the trash, doing his homework, putting dirty clothes in the hamper, going to the toilet on his own, or mowing the lawn with few or no reminders by his parents.

SHAPING OR SUCCESSIVE APPROXIMATIONS

Getting a child to do something he or she has never done before can be very frustrating to a parent. The child may refuse to take even the tiniest initial step like getting into the water when the parent is trying to teach the child to swim. Frequently, the dialogue goes like this:

MOTHER: Debbie, jump to me, I'll catch you.
DEBBIE: No.
MOTHER: Let me lift you into the water.
DEBBIE: No.
MOTHER: Put your toe in.
DEBBIE: No.
MOTHER: I'm not going to bring you to the pool again.

It is not at all unusual for the mother to become angry, the child upset, and the relationship between them to deteriorate.

One way to help the child learn a new behavior consists of first deciding on what the actual ultimate behavior is that is desired. In the above example, the desired behavior is swimming. Other examples would be riding a bike, urinating in the toilet, eating with a fork, and so forth. After defining the ultimate behavior desired, it is necessary to break the ultimate behavior into tiny steps, specifically defining each. The steps, then, are treated as separate behaviors and taught in the way discussed earlier. It is important that the first step be a simple one and something the child can easily do. When the child performs that behavior, he is then reinforced for that tiny step. Once there has been a substantial increase in that first behavior, the next step should be encouraged and reinforced. This would continue until the ultimate behavior desired is exhibited. This is called shaping or successive approximation.

An example will help clarify the concept. The study in which the child drops a ball into a box and a piece of candy is given has been cited. How did the child learn to drop the ball in the hole initially? One way, of course, is to tell the child to drop the ball in the hole and see what happens. Once he or she starts, the piece of candy given positively reinforces that behavior so it increases in frequency. "Dropping the ball in the hole" can also be viewed as a behavior the child does not initially have but which must be developed gradually. Suppose that a nursery schooler is brought into a large playroom in which a variety of toys and equipment are available. Also assume that in one corner of the room is the ball-dropping apparatus. The child is told that while he is in the room the overhead light will flash off occasionally. Each time it does, he will be told, he will receive a piece of candy. During the first day, the child will be observed closely. If he turns his head toward the ball-dropping apparatus in the corner of the room, then the person running the study will turn off the overhead light briefly. Looking toward the apparatus will be reinforced and the child will look more and more in that direction. Suppose the child were allowed to stay in the room ten minutes per day and each day the same procedures would be followed. During the end of the first day's session, he would be looking more and more in the direction of the apparatus more frequently, and at the end of the day, he would be given pieces of candy equivalent to the number of times the light had been flashed off. At the start of the second day's session, the light would be flashed again when he looked toward the apparatus. Later in the session, a change would be made. He would then be reinforced (i.e., light flashed) for taking a step in the direction of the apparatus; he would not be reinforced for just looking in that direction. Again at the end of the session, he would be given a piece of candy each time the light had been turned off. Sometime during the third session, he would have to take two steps in the direction of the apparatus in order to be reinforced. This procedure would be followed until eventually he was at the stage of picking up the ball and dropping it in the hole and, at that point, he would be reinforced by the apparatus itself.

The procedure followed consisted of defining the behavior ultimately desired (dropping the ball into the hole). Then a behavior was found that had a high likelihood of occurring (looking in the direction of the apparatus) which was a beginning toward the ultimate desired behavior. This latter behavior—looking toward the apparatus—was reinforced each time it occurred until it took place frequently. Then a behavior closer to the ultimate one, taking a step in that direction, was required before a reinforcement was given. Later extinction would be applied to taking a single step toward the apparatus. Instead, two or three steps would be required before a reinforcement was given. The person conducting the study must be alert so that the new behavior is required and reinforced at just the right time. If the procedure is too rapid, the child will not move on and learn the next step; if the procedure is too slow, the child will not be progressing toward the ultimate behavior at a speed which he is capable of achieving. Fortunately, if an error is made, it can always be corrected. In the case where the pace is too rapid, it is necessary to go back a few steps (e.g., back to looking toward the apparatus) and then begin again. When the pace has been too slow, little harm has been done other than time wasted.

Another shaping procedure is used with children learning to color in coloring books. The ultimate desired behavior is to have the child color within the lines. Initially, the child responds to the printed picture as if it were nonexistent and scribbles on the picture. Parents say how well the child has done and, in effect, reinforce the coloring behavior. Over time, the parents reinforce behavior that conforms more and more to staying within the lines until, ultimately, the child will be consistently coloring within the lines. Again, notice the parents first defined the ultimate behavior, then reinforced any behavior that represented a start in the right direction.

FADING

There is another procedure used to help children develop a new behavior and, as with some of the other principles presented, it is one that has been used by the general public. In essence, the procedure consists of initially helping the child accomplish almost all of the ultimate behaviors desired and then gradually reducing the amount of help given until the child is completing the behavior by himself. Thus, a parent could hold a child's hand while he or she uses a pair of scissors. Over time, the helping hand will be reduced until the child is cutting by himself. This is called a fading procedure (the fading of the helping hand). In teaching a child to hit a baseball, a parent frequently follows the same procedure. The parent stands behind the child with his arms circled around the child while the child holds onto the bat. At first, the parent exerts most of the effort in swinging the bat while the child holds. With continued experience, the parent gradually allows the child to swing and eventually the parent's hands are completely removed. The child by then is swinging the bat by himself. While it has not been stressed, the fading procedure involves reinforcement. This may be verbal reinforcement given by the parent or the observation of a successfully completed task.

CHAINING

A third technique used to help children learn some new behavior occurs when the child learns several distinct behaviors and then puts them together to perform the ultimate desired behavior. Printing one's name can be thought of as the printing of several different letters. A child might work on "P's" one day, then "A's," then "T's" and "Y's." The next step is to chain them together to spell Patty and the child will have reached the desired goal. Another example is swimming. The child must learn three different behaviors: (1) kicking the feet, (2) stroking the arms and (3) breathing properly. These three behaviors must be put together for the ultimate behavior—swimming—to take place.

MODELING OR IMITATION

A fourth way to instill a new behavior is also one that has been used before. Much of a child's learning comes from observing others. The little girl will frequently pretend to vacuum because she has seen her mother do it. The fact that children imitate others is something that can be of help when teaching a child a new behavior. In fact, parents frequently do just that when they say, "Watch me," or "Do it this way." Anyone teaching someone a new behavior will almost always demonstrate how it is done. One use of this procedure has been in toilet-training problems. In some families, the child to be trained has not seen his parents use the toilet. Having been deprived of this experience the child finds learning much more difficult. This procedure is referred to as modeling (i.e., following a model) or imitation.

OVERLAPPING OF TECHNIQUES

While these various techniques to initiate a new behavior have been presented separately, the alert reader can see that there is overlap. Thus, in chaining, successive approximation or fading could be used in developing each step. Modeling could take place at the beginning and then be followed by fading. The important point is that the child should learn the behavior.

EXERCISES: INITIATION OF BEHAVIORS

Below are some new behaviors that parents might desire in their children. Look at each one and think of the various procedures that could be used to help children learn them.

1. *Catching a ball*

2 *Dialing a phone number*

3. *Making a bed*

4. *Telling time*

5. *Learning the alphabet*

6. *Riding a bike*

MAINTENANCE OF BEHAVIORS

Let's now look at the third part of the curve (part C) in Figure 28, which shows that the desired behavior continues to be displayed at a consistent rate. The child now regularly makes his bed, takes out the trash, picks up his clothes, or does his homework. This is referred to as the maintenance of the behavior. Parents, when first introduced to behavioral methods, are frequently concerned about giving candy or other tangible reinforcers to their children because they feel that their children will forever need to be reinforced. In a toilet-training study to be presented in detail in Chapter Eleven, a child was given an after-dinner mint for urinating in the toilet. Individuals told about this study sometimes responded as if they felt the child would have to have a mint each time he urinated for the rest of his life. Obviously, that would neither be reasonable nor economically feasible. Individuals doing behavior modification work are always most concerned about having the tangible reinforcers eliminated and parents' involvement decreased as the child continues to emit the desired behavior.

How then is this accomplished? There are two techniques usually applied that are effective in eliminating tangible reinforcers and reducing the effort put forth by the parents. Remember that to help the child perform the behavior regularly, he or she should be reinforced immediately after the behavior takes place, *each time* it occurs. Once the behavior has been learned well, as indicated by its frequency, it is then possible to modify the reinforcement. For example, the reader will recall the box in which the child dropped a ball in the top and a piece of candy fell into the plastic dish. If a child were introduced to that apparatus and he dropped the ball and received the candy, his ball-dropping behavior would increase. Assume that each day for a period of fifteen minutes, the child was allowed to operate the machine. After a few days, he would probably be picking up the ball and dropping it in again at a rapid rate, probably as many times as physically possible during a fifteen-minute period. His rate of responding would not be increasing; the charting of such frequency would be represented by a straight horizontal line. This flat line represents the maintenance of the behavior. Once the child has reached this maintenance stage, it is possible to begin to reduce the number of reinforcements given.

The first step in this reduction could be giving a reinforcement for two responses rather than one. The child would drop in the ball and candy would not be forthcoming but the next time he dropped the ball, he would receive a piece of candy. From then on, for a time, only every other response would be reinforced. After awhile, the schedule could be changed so that the child would be required to drop the ball in three times to get a piece of candy. Even later, four responses would be required before the candy is given. In this manner, more and more responses are required for the reinforcement. This is one technique in which there can be a reduction in the number of reinforcements without a decrease in the behavior's frequency.

FIXED- AND VARIABLE-RATIO SCHEDULES

The procedure described above in which a certain number of responses are required to receive a reinforcement is called a fixed-ratio schedule (i.e., so many responses per one reinforcement). The fixed schedule technique is much more likely to take place in laboratories where each response can be counted. What is likely to take place in the home or in the school is a variable-ratio schedule. To illustrate the variable-ratio schedule, let's look again at the ball-dropping apparatus. Instead of giving the candy after the second or third response (using variable ratio reinforcement), the reinforcement is given after three responses, then two, then five, then six, then one. In other words, the number of responses required for a reinforcement varies.

REDUCTION OF PARENT INVOLVEMENT

The parents' ultimate desire, of course, is to have the child show the desired behavior with relatively little need for their involvement. For example, parents would like to see the child make his bed, take out the trash, tidy his room, get a haircut, and do his homework pretty much on his own. If the procedures that have been cited are followed, this can be achieved. Initially, reinforcement must be given *each time* the task is performed until it takes place regularly. Then the reinforcement can be withheld every so often but the behavior will persist. Gradually the number of reinforcements can be reduced further and the behavior will still be maintained. Care should be taken not to move too rapidly in the reduction of reinforcement or extinction may take place. If extinction does start, more generous reinforcements should be effective in reinstating the desired behavior.

FIXED- AND VARIABLE-INTERVAL SCHEDULES

Another procedure for reducing the number of reinforcements is probably more applicable to a laboratory than the home but is worth mentioning. Our ball-dropping box, again, can provide an illustration. Assume that the child has been using the box regularly and receiving a piece of candy each time the ball is dropped and you want more responses per reinforcement. The inside of the apparatus can be so designed that once the child has been reinforced, it will be ten seconds before the next reinforcement is available. Any response (i.e., dropping the ball) that occurs before the ten seconds are up is not reinforced, only the response that occurs after ten seconds have elapsed is reinforced. If the responses keep taking place, it is possible to extend the time to fifteen seconds or later to twenty seconds. In this manner, only some of the responses are being reinforced but the behavior of ball-dropping persists. If the time that must elapse before the next response is reinforced remains constant, this procedure is called fixed-interval schedule. As with the variable-ratio schedule, the interval can change after each reinforced response (for example, five seconds, sixteen seconds, four seconds, nine seconds, and so on). This is called a variable-interval schedule.

With careful observation and by following one of the schedules mentioned above, many behaviors will be emitted for a single reinforcement. One gradually can require more and more time for each reinforcement. When the reinforcement is only given on a weekly basis, the effort that must be expanded by the parent is negligible. For all practical purposes, the child performs the desired tasks on his own.

THE IMPORTANCE OF VERBAL REINFORCEMENT

While the use of tangible reinforcers is quite important in establishing a behavior, there is another approach that will help children exhibit particular behaviors independently. To bring this about, each time the child performs a desired task and is reinforced, the parent should also verbally reinforce the child. Thus, each time the child performs the desired behavior, the parent might say "Good" or "I'm pleased with what you have done." Ginott (1965) has stated that a parent should always comment favorably on how well the task was done rather than saying "Good boy" or "Good girl." We believe that either might be verbally reinforcing and no evidence shows the superiority of either approach. If a verbal reinforcement is coupled with a tangible reinforcer on each occasion, over time the verbal reinforcer becomes as effective as the tangible reinforcer. As the behavior becomes more routine for the child, a verbal reinforcement from the parent is all that is needed to reinforce it and with even more time, the verbal reinforcement can be fixed on some ratio schedule so it is given infrequently. When this stage is reached, the events seem to approximate closely the situation in everyday life in which things are done in an adequate manner and every so often someone tells us that we've done a good job.

DISCRIMINATION

One concept important in understanding children is called discrimination—when the child can tell the difference between two objects or events. Discrimination is a behavioral term in that one can tell if the child can make the discrimination by testing to see if he or she knows it. How the child learns to make a discrimination is shown in the following example. Assume we had a piece of equipment (see Figure 29) so designed that two figures could be presented—a triangle and a circle. The triangle and the circle could be alternated on either side so the child would not learn to respond to one side only. Underneath each figure would be a button the child could push to indicate which figure he chose.

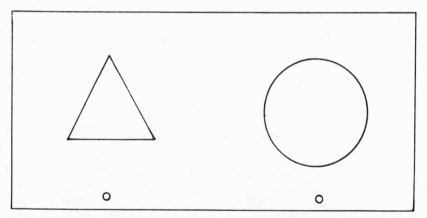

Figure 29. Apparatus to illustrate discrimination.

On the side of the equipment would be a dish into which candy could be dropped when the child pushed a button. Let us so arrange the equipment so that each time the child pressed the button under the circle, a piece of candy fell into the dish. If the button under the triangle were pressed, no candy would fall into the dish. Remember that the circle is sometimes on the right and sometimes on the left so the child does not learn to push only the button on the right.

If a child were allowed to play with this piece of equipment each day, over a period of time he would tend to push the button under the circle more and more and that under the triangle less and less. If we plot the percentages of presses under the triangle and under the circle each day, we could see the changes illustrated in Figure 30. Eventually the child would be pressing only the button under the circle. We could then say that the child had learned to discriminate between the triangle and the circle.

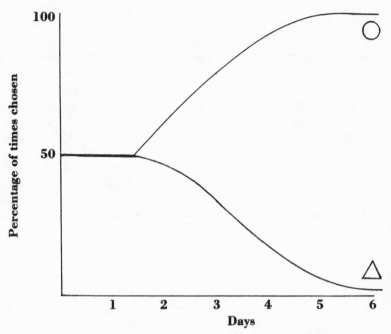

Figure 30. Percentage of time triangle or circle was chosen.

One of the most important steps in the learning process for children is being able to discriminate objects, events, colors, tones, shapes, time, and so forth. A careful observation of a child's behavior will reveal that he will make many discriminations and observations each day over time and he will also reveal how he learns to make them. One example, pointed out by a student some time ago, concerned a child about three who had just learned to use the toilet. His parents were having a party when the child rushed in shouting, "Mommy, I have to go to the toilet." The guests tittered and the mother took the child to the toilet. Later the mother explained to the child that when guests were present, the child should whisper his toilet needs in his mother's ear. If no one other than family were present, however, the child could speak out loud. Stated another way, the child had to learn to discriminate between guests in the home and no guests in the home. The two different behaviors called for are much the same as the two different behaviors required in the laboratory when the child was confronted with a triangle and a circle.

Another example of behavior frequently found in most families involves a situation in which the mother asks the child to perform certain tasks. The child, engrossed in playing, does not respond. The mother may ask again and still no response. The next time the mother asks, the tone of her voice will be a little firmer, the pitch a little higher, and the words a little stronger and more forceful. When the mother speaks in this manner, the child jumps up to do the task. The child, over time, has learned that there aren't any serious consequences for not responding when his mother asks him to do something in a nice way. If, however, she sounds more serious, there are certain consequences if compliance is not forthcoming. The child has made a discrimination between the different ways in which a mother asks for compliance. Mothers who have taught this lesson well frequently say things like, "The only way I can get that child to obey is to yell at him."

STIMULUS CONTROL

Another way of discussing discrimination is to say that a child comes under the stimulus control of an object. Thus, the object exerts stimulus control over the child. In the example cited earlier, in which the child discriminated between a circle and triangle, it could be said that the child is now controlled by the stimulus of the circle, i.e., he pushes the button under the circle when the circle appears along side of the triangle. Discrimination can be viewed in terms of stimulus control. When a mother says, "Come here this instant" and the child comes, he is said to be under stimulus control of the mother's command. The stimulus control concept can be noticed particularly in nursery or elementary school. With some teachers, children are quick to respond when asked to do something. Other teachers have great difficulty controlling their classes; the children may talk and in general do not pay attention to the teacher. While particular events and objects control behavior, children are also controlled by time. They learn that a certain time is associated with certain activities, such as eating, going to bed, getting up, and so on.

EXERCISES: DISCRIMINATION

Consider some of the discriminations a child (preferably your own) might make in the following circumstances:

1. Getting up in the morning

2. Dressing

3. Eating breakfast

4. Playing with toys

5. Watching TV

CONCEPT FORMATION AND STIMULUS CONTROL

Concept formation can be viewed in terms of stimulus control. Concept formation is usually thought of as some inner process but it can also be understood in terms of dimensions of a series of stimuli. Concepts such as "larger" and "smaller" are often referred to as if the child had the concept mastered, i.e., he understands that some things are larger or smaller than other things. A behavioral approach, however, focuses on the "things" or stimuli involved. In an example similar to the one in which the child discriminated between a circle and a triangle, the same equipment can be used to teach the child to discriminate between larger and smaller. Let's assume that two stimuli are presented to the child as illustrated in Figure 31.

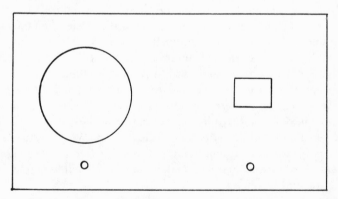

Figure 31. Apparatus for testing concept of larger and smaller.

Again the child must press a button under one of the figures. If he presses the one under the circle, a piece of candy is given; if he presses the button under the square, nothing happens. Notice that there are two dimensions involved—the two figures differ in shape as well as in size. We could paint them different colors so that they would differ three ways. If the next two figures presented were those shown in Figure 32, and we were interested in teaching larger or smaller, we would reinforce the pressing of the button under the large square. Obviously,

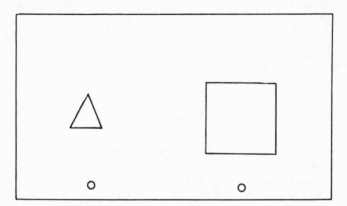

Figure 32. Another example of testing the concept of larger and smaller.

if numerous other combinations were presented and the larger figure was always reinforced, the child would eventually learn the concepts of larger and smaller. Stated another way, the child would learn to select out one dimension (that of size) and respond to it and it alone. Other concepts are learned in similar ways in everyday life. Learning the concepts of "left" and "right" is something children master over time. The complex concept of telling time is another.

EXERCISES: CONCEPT FORMATION

Consider other concepts that are learned by children in this gradual manner by selecting out a dimension or dimensions and responding to it.

1. How to say "Daddy"

2. Learning the colors of crayons

3. The weight of objects

4. The temperature outdoors

5. The names of coins

CUES AND DISCRIMINATIVE STIMULI

In several places in the book reference has been made to the cue preceding a particular behavior. It was referred to in the mother's calling the child in for a spanking, an example of negative reinforcement. It was also referred to in the discrimination apparatus when the circle and triangle were presented. The cue for pushing the button under the circle is the circle itself. These stimuli that serve as cues are called discriminative stimuli (S^D). If a mother says, "Do it now" or "Stop," this is an S^D for the child to do it now or stop.

DEALING WITH FEARS AND ANXIETIES

One other concept that parents should be familiar with concerns the fears or anxieties children have. This was referred to in discussing respondent behavior. Some stimuli, which have been associated with pain, now evoke anxiety or fear. Anxiety and fear were defined as changes in heartbeat, stomach contractions, breathing rate, and so forth. A child who has been chased by a dog will later display fearful behavior when any dog comes into sight. Parents should be sensitive to the fact that their children may also be anxious or fearful about performing some task the parents want them to perform. If anxiety is involved, then it is important to reduce it gradually. This is best accomplished by proceeding in a manner similar to successive approximations. The child should be exposed to the fearful situation for only a short time or exposed to it from a physical distance, and then be removed. Gradually increase the time exposed, or the distance, until the fear is reduced. It is important to positively reinforce the child each time exposure takes place. Thus, a child who is afraid of reciting a poem in front of company should be asked first to speak a sentence in front of the family. He should then be told how well he did; no criticism should be given. Later he could recite a short poem in front of the family and later, a longer poem.

Parents should keep in mind the interrelationship between respondent and operant behavior. A child, frightened by some event, may find that by mentioning his fear, he has found another way to get parental attention. We are familiar with a little girl who was afraid of fire sirens. Perhaps this came from some exposure to the piercing sound of the siren. The parents, in an attempt to reduce this fear, took the child to visit the local fire station and bought her books and toys about fires and fire engines. The fear did not go away, however; it grew stronger. The child had learned that any mention of fire brought attention from the parents.

Exercises: Fears and Anxieties

Consider how a child could be gradually exposed to fearful stimuli and consequently have them reduced:

1. *Fear of cats*

2. *Afraid to go to school*

3. *Afraid to go down a slide*

4. *Afraid to pick up a worm*

5. *Fear of strange persons*

Summary

This chapter presented ways to initiate desired behaviors and how to maintain the behaviors without reinforcement each time they occur. Shaping, successive approximation, fading, chaining, modeling, and imitation were discussed. In maintenance of behavior, the use of fixed- and variable-interval schedules, fixed- and variable-ratio schedules was also presented. The importance of verbal reinforcers was stressed. The concepts of discrimination, stimulus control, concept formation, cues, and discriminative stimuli were introduced. Finally, it was shown that fears and anxieties can be dealt with using the behavioral approach.

Chapter 7

An Overview

So far, we have tried to present a new way of looking at and understanding children. In the preceding chapters, techniques were presented that are capable of changing behavior as the parent desires—either by reducing the frequency of undesirable behavior or increasing the frequency of desirable behavior. Examples have been given that serve to clarify these concepts. The purpose of this chapter is to summarize the material and to present an outline of the steps parents might take when confronted by a problem with their child.

APPLICATION OF THE BEHAVIORAL APPROACH TO PROBLEM BEHAVIOR

There are several points that should precede the presentation of such examples. One is that the behavioral approach can be applied if some behavior of the child, or lack of it, becomes disturbing to the parents. Most of the time, a child's behavior is considered satisfactory by the parents. Obviously, if a particular child's behavior is quite deviant, there are many areas in which he misbehaves but such a child is unusual. When most parents feel they have a "problem child," it is because the child's behavior is upsetting to them in only one or two areas. For a parent to use the behavioral approach, there must be some behavior of concern to them. If such parents find themselves in a position in which there are many different behaviors of concern, they should select one behavior to work on at a time and continue to behave in the same way toward the other deviant behaviors as they have in the past.

DEFINING THE TARGET BEHAVIOR

The first step, then, is to decide on one certain behavior of concern. This is sometimes referred to as the target behavior. It is important to define this behavior as precisely and as carefully as possible. Some clear-cut definitions are: thumb-sucking, hitting one's sibling, bed-wetting, not putting toys away, yelling, not eating vegetables, not going to bed on time, and not doing homework. Some definitions not at all clear are: immature behavior, showing insecurity, being overly aggressive or emotional. The definitions must be precise so that others will understand what is meant; the communication must be clear. One way to check on this, after a behavior has been defined, is to ask someone else (perhaps one's spouse) if he or she understands the definition. If possible, both should watch the child as he or she displays the behavior in question so that both agree on what it is and when it is taking place.

RECORDING FREQUENCY

Once the behavior has been selected and precisely defined, the next step consists of determining how frequently it occurs. Some procedure for recording must be developed that gives an accurate picture of the frequency of the behavior and is not too great a burden for the recorder. Record-keeping is important. One should determine in advance *how* the behavior is to be recorded and for *how long*. If the behavior is one that occurs only in one room, the recording can take place there. If the behavior takes place in several rooms or outside, then some portable recording procedure is necessary. This can be accomplished by using a piece of paper and a pencil, also a stop-watch or tally recorder. To keep the recording from becoming a chore, decide on a specific period of time to be spent in observing and recording. Thus, if thumb-sucking is viewed as a problem and the child sucks his or her thumb quite frequently, it would be an all-consuming task to follow the child around all day to observe and record. However, a one-hour or a half-hour period in the afternoon could be set aside for observation. In some cases, where it is important to have some record throughout the day, periods of ten minutes duration or so can be scheduled. The total observation time may be an hour or two with ten minutes here and there, but for the most part the whole day is sampled.

After a procedure for recording the behavior has been decided upon, the recording should begin. While it may be difficult to do, it is important to continue to behave toward the child in the same way as before as far as the behavior in question is concerned. The only difference is that the behavior, when it takes place, is being recorded. It is possible that the child will notice that his or her behavior is being recorded. If this happens, the parent can say, for example, "We are concerned about your wetting the bed and we want to help you with this problem. Right now we're just keeping track of how often you wet the bed. Later we'll try to help you stop." Any behavior could be substituted for bed-wetting. And one advantage of a behavioral approach is that parents can be quite open and frank with their child about a behavior that concerns them and what steps are to be taken. Some examples of data recording would be:

1. A small card is taped by the toilet. Each line is dated and each time the child urinates in the toilet, a tally is made next to the appropriate date.

2. Each afternoon from four to five the mother unobtrusively observes her son or daughter. Each time he puts his thumb in his mouth, the mother times it with a stop-watch. At the end of the hour, the mother knows how many minutes out of that hour the child had his thumb in his mouth.

3. A child uses "dirty" words. (The specific words are labeled "dirty" by the mother). Each time the mother hears her child use such a word she makes a mark on the calendar. At the end of the week she knows how many such words her child used.

The record should be kept for several days depending upon the behavior being observed. Typically at least a week is recommended, although sometimes five days will suffice if the behavior is associated with school activity (e.g., homework). The reason for collecting this data is to see how severe the problem is in terms of its frequency, and so it can be determined if any change has taken place. In order to make a comparison, it is sometimes necessary to take the recorded data and to plot it on a graph. Thus, one might have plotted the minutes a child sucks his thumb during a one-hour period or the number of times he has had to go to the toilet during the day.

DETERMINING THE TREATMENT TECHNIQUE

After collecting data on the frequency of the behavior, one can determine what changes are to be made. The first step is a careful analysis of the behavior as well as the events that take place *before* and *after* the behavior. It may be observed, for example, that the parent is maintaining some undesirable behavior by reinforcing the child with attention. Thus, to reduce the frequency of that behavior, the parent can apply extinction. The observation period also provides time to ascertain what reinforcers would probably be most effective with the child. As stated earlier, it is usually appropriate, and most effective, if several techniques are applied at once. One may wish to use extinction on an undesirable behavior, a time-out if the behavior is extreme, and positive reinforcement for a behavior that is incompatible with the undesirable behavior. Successive approximations or chaining techniques may be required, as well as the teaching of some kind of discrimination.

APPLYING THE TREATMENT TECHNIQUE

After the treatment technique has been decided, it should be put into effect and, once put into effect, it should be followed consistently. If extinction is to be used to reduce temper-tantrum behavior, each time the child has a temper tantrum, he or she should be ignored. If the child is to be reinforced following some behavior, he should be reinforced each time he behaves appropriately. The recording of the frequency of behavior should be continued as meticulously as before. The application of the treatment is frequently a difficult time for parents. This difficulty seems to occur for two reasons: One, the amount of time and effort the parents take to apply the treatment and continue to record the data; and two, when a parent starts behaving differently toward the child (i.e., the treatment), the child will frequently change his behavior and produce even more undesirable behavior. This, of course, is the child's way of attempting to control the parent and, not infrequently, he or she is successful. For example, the child may be whining and crying to get something he or she wants. The parents want to reduce this crying and whining, and when they institute some treatment, the child reacts by throwing temper tantrums. The parent then stops the treatment by saying that it is obviously better to have the child whine and cry than to throw temper tantrums. The child is obviously in control of the situation. Thus, a change in the child's behavior—a change showing more deviant behavior—is not unusual. Fortunately, the new behavior is not as well learned as the old and if it is not reinforced, it will cease in a short time. Stated another way, if the parent can withstand this brief spurt of deviant behavior, it will disappear. One thing for certain, a different behavior, although more irritating, does show that the treatment is having an effect.

RULES FOR FACILITATING BEHAVIOR CHANGE

Which treatment to apply has been described earlier and varies a great deal depending upon the situation. While these treatment techniques have been described separately, it is not uncommon for several to be applied at one time to a particular problem. Thus, one may want to ignore an undesirable behavior (extinction) and, at the same time, reinforce some incompatible behavior. By using two or more techniques simultaneously, there is a greater likelihood of success as well as of a shorter period of time needed.

REDUCING A PROBLEM BEHAVIOR

Let's first view the situation when an attempt is being made to reduce a behavior. Check first to see if attention is in any way maintaining the behavior; this can be done by ignoring the behavior and seeing what happens. If attention is a factor, there should be a decrease in the frequency of that behavior. Also to be watched for is a change in behavior when the child learns that the old behavior doesn't work any longer in getting attention. Second, a time-out should be considered. The time-out room or area should contain little that might be reinforcing for the child and he should spend only a few minutes there when the undesirable behavior occurs. Rules should be spelled out clearly to the child so that he or she knows that when the undesirable behavior occurs, he or she will have to spend a certain amount of time in the time-out room (probably the child's own room). Last, some behavior of the child that is incompatible with the undesired behavior should be found and positively reinforced. An increase in such behavior obviously means a decrease in the undesired behavior. These general steps will usually be effective with most undesirable behaviors.

INCREASING FREQUENCY OF BEHAVIOR

If one is interested in increasing the frequency of a behavior, first it is necessary to determine whether or not the behavior is capable of being performed by the child. If not, it may be necessary to build the behavior through successive approximations. The various steps should be figured out and developed logically, and the child reinforced for each step. When the final step is reached, that behavior should also be reinforced so that it is well established. Chaining may be required if the behavior is fairly complex. The reinforcement to be used should be carefully determined. Certainly one good procedure is to take some activity the child enjoys and then encourage him to earn it by collecting tokens or tallies for displaying the desirable behavior. In one previous example, a little girl earned a surprise on Saturday if she made her bed a certain number of times a week. The surprise consisted of a trip to the zoo, candy, a toy, or a trip with her mother.

SOME FINAL CONSIDERATIONS

It is most important, as stated earlier, to continue to record the frequency of the behavior. One should not expect abrupt changes in frequency; often the behavior has been practiced for years so it can hardly be expected that changes will come about in just a few days. However, depending on the behavior, one should expect positive results after a few weeks. If this does not happen, it is necessary to reanalyze the behavior and the approach used. For undesirable behavior, one should check to see if some thing or someone else is reinforcing the behavior and, thereby, maintaining it. For desirable behavior, one should determine if the reinforcer is effective and if it is being given consistently. Is the behavior something that the child is not capable of doing? Have the steps in the successive approximations been too great? After such analysis, some new change in the treatment should take place. In our experience, it has seldom been necessary to change the procedure more than once.

Remember to be both consistent and persistent. It is well known that the procedures outlined above involve hard work and are time consuming. In the long run, however, not only will there be a saving of time, but the child will be better adjusted and the parents much happier. It is important to insure that the desired behavior is maintained and the old behaviors do not return. This requires a certain vigilance on the part of the parents so that their own behavior does not revert to the old ways. Remember, each day that passes in which the child does not show his old undesired behavior, the less likelihood there is that it will ever return. Similarly, the longer the child shows the desired behavior, the greater the likelihood that it will remain a permanent behavior. In summary then the steps to follow are:

1. A clear definition of the ultimate desired behavior

2. Some way to measure how frequently the behavior of concern takes place

3. A way of treating the problem and bringing about a change in the behavior of concern and

4. Continued recording to see if successful, and if not, a change to some other behavioral technique.

After completing this book and the exercises, you now possess a new way to understand and modify a child's behavior. When a problem arises, you have the option of using the method used before or implementing the one described in this book. We believe that by using the behavioral method, you will become more familiar with it and find it extremely useful. We are also aware that learning is much more complicated than described and that family interaction by itself is quite complex. Consequently, the techniques described may not be effective in some cases. We strongly suggest that, if some problem resists the behavioral approach or any of the other techniques known, a child expert be consulted. The sooner undesirable behavior is eliminated, the better for the child, the better for family interaction, and the greater the ease with which such behavior can be removed. The longer undesirable behavior persists, the more difficult it is to change.

This section includes research articles written by psychologists and others to illustrate the procedures and principles presented in the first section. These papers were selected because they represented a variety of problems encountered by reasonably normal parents dealing with normal children. They may be of more interest to students in the field than parents, but the level of the material is not difficult if one is familiar with the concepts and procedures covered earlier. One will notice that the procedures for each study are essentially the same: a clear definition of the behavior of concern; a way of recording the frequency of the behavior; an experimental analysis of the situation; a technique to increase or decrease the frequency of the behavior; and continuous recording to determine if the treatment is effective. You are encouraged to think ahead of each author and attempt to devise other behavioral procedures that might be equally effective.

Chapter 8

The Elimination of Temper Tantrum Behavior by Extinction Procedures[1]

Carl D. Williams

This paper reports the successful treatment of tyrant-like tantrum behavior in a male child by the removal of reinforcement. The subject (S) was approximately 21 months old. He had been seriously ill much of the first 18 months of his life. His health then improved considerably, and he gained weight and vigor.

S now demanded the special care and attention that had been given him over the many critical months. He enforced some of his wishes, especially at bedtime, by unleashing tantrum behavior to control the actions of his parents.

The parents and aunt took turns in putting him to bed both at night and for S's afternoon nap. If the parent left the bedroom after putting S in his bed, S would scream and fuss until the parent returned to the room. As a result, the parent was unable to leave the bedroom until after S went to sleep. If the parent began to read while in the bedroom, S would cry until the reading material was put down. The parents felt that S enjoyed his control over them and that he fought off going to sleep as long as he could. In any event, a parent was spending from one-half to two hours each bedtime just waiting in the bedroom until S went to sleep.

Following medical reassurance regarding S's physical condition, it was decided to remove the reinforcement of this tyrant-like tantrum behavior. Consistent with the learning principle that, in general, behavior that is not reinforced will be extinguished, a parent or the aunt put S to bed in a leisurely and relaxed fashion. After bedtime pleasantries, the parent left the bedroom and closed the

[1]Reprinted with permission from the *Journal of Abnormal and Social Psychology* 59 (1959): 269.

door. S screamed and raged, but the parent did not re-enter the room. The duration of screaming and crying was obtained from the time the door was closed.

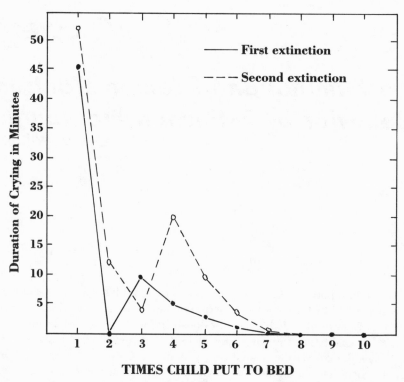

Figure 1. Length of crying in two extinction series as a function of successive occasions of being put to bed

The results are shown in Figure 1. It can be seen that S continued screaming for 45 min. the first time he was put to bed in the first extinction series. S did not cry at all the second time he was put to bed. This is perhaps attributable to his fatigue from the crying of Occasion 1. By the tenth occasion, S no longer whimpered, or cried when the parent left the room. Rather, he smiled as they left. The parents felt that he made happy sounds until he dropped off to sleep.

About a week later, S screamed and fussed after the aunt put him to bed, probably reflecting spontaneous recovery of the tantrum behavior. The aunt then reinforced the tantrum behavior by returning to S's bedroom and remaining there until he went to sleep. It was then necessary to extinguish his behavior a second time.

Figure 1 shows that the second extinction curve is similar to the first. Both curves are generally similar to extinction curves obtained with subhuman subjects. The second extinction series reached zero by the ninth occasion. No further tantrums at bedtime were reported during the next two years.

It should be emphasized that the treatment in this case did not involve aversive punishment. All that was done was to remove the reinforcement. Extinction of the tyrant-like tantrum behavior then occurred.

No unfortunate side or aftereffects of this treatment were observed. At three and three-quarters years of age, S appeared to be a friendly, expressive, outgoing child.

Chapter 9

A Case Study in Discrimination Learning[1]
Donald K. Pumroy and Shirley S. Pumroy

A. INTRODUCTION

This case study provides a conditioning paradigm illustrating the solution to a specific problem in child-rearing. The problem arose in the following manner. When the subject was approximately 20 months of age, he would begin to call "Mommy" or "Daddy" on awakening. This call was to inform the *E*s he was ready to get up and to begin his day's activities. He, naturally, would awaken at different times and his calling would continue until he was allowed to get up. On the days when he would awaken early this was disturbing to the *E*s. On some occasions one of the *E*s would enter the room and tell the child it was not time to get up. Sometimes the child would go back to sleep, but on some days he would wait for 10 to 15 minutes and begin to call again. The *E*s decided that what was desired was to have the child call when he was ready to get up and, thus, be allowed sufficient sleep, but that he should not call until eight o'clock. The problem, thus analyzed, lent itself to a discrimination learning situation.

B. METHOD

1. SUBJECT

The subject was a healthy normal male child who was 21 months old at the start of the study.

[1]Reprinted with permission from *The Journal of Genetic Psychology* 110 (1967): 87–89.

2. PROCEDURES

The response used was the number of times "Mommy" or "Daddy" was called. On Day 1, 2, and 3 when the S arose before eight o'clock he was allowed to call until eight o'clock at which time one of the E s went into his room and picked him up. On each day the number of calls that he made was tallied. On Day 4, the same procedure was followed except that at eight o'clock a small lamp was lit in the S's room. This lamp consisted of a small white night light (7½-watt bulb), similar to Christmas tree lights. The light was situated approximately five feet from the crib and at the S's eye level and in his line of vision when he would stand up and call. On Day 4, at eight o'clock, the light was turned on by the E plugging in an extension cord outside of the room. As soon as the S called "Mommy" or "Daddy" after the light was on, the E entered the room to get him up. The E then said, "It's time to get up. When the light comes on it's okay to get up." On subsequent days the light would be turned on at eight o'clock and as soon as the S said "Mommy" or "Daddy" after the light came on one of the E's would enter the room and get him up. Thus the calling of "Mommy" or "Daddy" was rewarded only when the light was on. On each day the number of calls of "Mommy" or "Daddy" prior to eight o'clock was tallied.

3. RESULTS

The results are presented in Figure 1. The number of calls per four-day blocks are plotted. Note that the curve drops following the introduction of the light, which indicates the S was learning to make the discrimination. On days 29 to 32 there were 101 responses made. In that four-day block, there were three days of zero responses and one day of 101 responses. That one day was preceded by a visit of the child's grandfather. The S's grandfather was not aware of or had forgotten about the experiment, so when the child called, the grandfather entered the room before the light could be turned on. The following day the child emitted 101 responses.

4. DISCUSSION

The collection of data terminated at the end of 68 days even though the curve was not asymptotic to zero. There are three possible reasons for the training not to be complete. One is that the number of calls is related to how long the subject sleeps. Thus if he sleeps past eight o'clock he would not call. Certainly the physiological condition of the S (hungry, wet, tired) would then have an effect on number of responses. The second reason is that there were stimuli other than

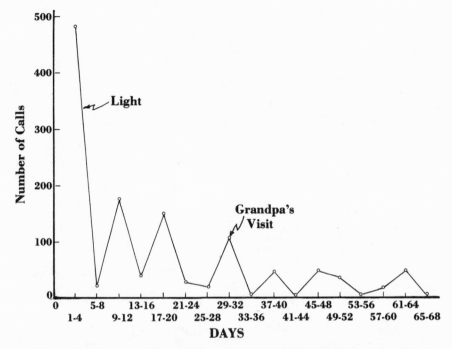

Figure 1. Number of Calls of "Mommy" or "Daddy" Per Four-Day Blocks

the light to which the *S* may have been responding: e.g., the sunshine coming into the room. Lastly the response of the subject (calling "Mommy" or "Daddy") was rewarded during the day when the light was not lit.

Note that the learning did take place without the use of any aversive stimuli. The light has continued to be used by the *E*s and the *S* has trained a younger sister to obey it. The *S* is now 6 and there appear to be no adverse side effects nor long-term effects as far as his behavior is concerned.

5. SUMMARY

The problem involved in this study arose when the *E*'s 21-month-old son would awaken early and call "Mommy" or "Daddy." The *E*s wanted *S* to call when ready to get up, but not before 8 A.M. The number of calls prior to 8 A.M. was recorded for four days. At 8 A.M. on the fourth day the *E*s lit a light in the *S*'s room. When the *S* called after 8 A.M. he was reinforced by one of the *E*s entering his room and taking him from his crib. Results show that the *S* learned the discrimination.

Chapter 10

Modification of Behavior Problems in the Home with a Parent as Observer and Experimenter[1]

R. Vance Hall, Saul Axelrod, Lucille Tyler, Ellen Grief, Fowler C. Jones, and Roberta Robertson

Four parents enrolled in a Responsive Teaching class carried out experiments using procedures they had devised for alleviating their children's problem behaviors. The techniques used involved different types of reinforcement, extinction, and punishment. One parent increased the frequency of the wearing of an orthodontic device during five daily time checks by making an immediate monetary payoff contingent on wearing the device. A second parent increased the number of points earned for doing daily household tasks by providing back-ups for which the points could be exchanged. The parents of a 4-yr-old boy decreased the frequency of whines, cries, and complaints by removing social attention when such behavior occurred. A mother decreased the duration of time it took for her 5-yr-old daughter to get dressed by making permission to watch television contingent on dressing within 30 min of the time she got up in the morning. Brief reversals of contingencies were used to show causal relationships between the procedures used and the changes in behavior. Checks on the reliability of measurement were made by persons present in the home.

Most behavior modification experiments have been conducted by sophisticated researchers in institutional, classroom, or laboratory settings. Some studies, however, have employed parents as therapists for their childrens' behavior problems and were carried on in the home environment (Hawkins,

[1]Reprinted with permission from the *Journal of Applied Behavior Analysis* 5 (1972): 53-64.

Peterson, Schweid, and Bijou, 1966; Zeilberger, Sampen, and Sloane, 1968; Wahler, 1969). The subjects for these experiments exhibited sufficiently severe behavior difficulties that they were referred to a psychological clinic. The children were then evaluated and their parents were given suggestions on the type of behavior modification procedures that might alleviate their children's problems. The data collection tasks were conducted by the experimenters or trained observers in the children's homes.

The present studies, in contrast, were originated and conducted by individuals (the third, fourth, fifth, and sixth authors) whose main exposure to operant conditioning principles was a Responsive Teaching course in which they were enrolled.

A more detailed description of the course that follows the Responsive Teaching Model is given in Hall and Copeland (1971). Essentially, however, participants in the Responsive Teaching course were enrolled for 3 hr of credit. The class met for a 3-hr session once each week for 16 weeks (one semester). Lectures, films, quizzes, and discussion groups of about 10 persons led by a graduate student leader were used to present basic information on recording and measurement, applied behavior analysis research designs, learning theory principles, and examples of studies carried out by researchers and by previous class members. The basic course content can be found in the *Behavior Management Series* (Hall, 1971). The participants carried out their studies, aided by the leader assigned to their group, during the semester in which they took the course. The number of participants in the classes varied from 40 to more than 70.

The studies presented were carried out in the home environment, dealt with relatively mild behavioral difficulties, and required no special apparatus. In each case, the experimenters served as the primary observer.

EXPERIMENT 1

SUBJECT AND SETTING

Jerry first started wearing an orthodontic device when he was 8 yr. old. The dental mechanism consisted of a removable head band held in place by a plastic band around his neck. Although the recommended wearing time was approximately 12 hr. a day, Jerry used the device only a few hours daily. After 2 yr., the orthodontist reported little improvement in Jerry's condition. A move to a new area resulted in a second type of removable orthodontic device that also contained two bands. Again, Jerry used the device less often than recommended. After 8 yr., four dentists, and approximately $3300 in dental fees, Jerry's orthodontic condition was essentially unchanged.

OBSERVATIONS

Five times a day, at varying intervals, Mrs. T. observed Jerry to determine whether or not he was wearing his orthodontic device. On week days the first of these observations occurred just before breakfast. One came after breakfast but before Jerry left for school in the morning. One came after Mrs. T. arrived home from school in the afternoon but before the evening meal. One came shortly after supper and one came within 30 min of bedtime. On weekends, checks were made before breakfast, between breakfast and lunch, after lunch but before supper, shortly after supper and within 30 min of bedtime. The exact times of the checks varied somewhat and Jerry did not know exactly when the checks would be made. If both bands were in place, Mrs. T. placed a "+" on a recording sheet. If not, she reported a "0". Mr. T. conducted reliability checks each weekend. On signal from Mrs. T. both observed whether or not the device was in place. Mrs. T. recorded a "+" or "0" on the sheet. Mr. T. then told her whether he had scored the observation as "+" or "0". Mrs. T. then noted Mr. T's observation on the chart. In all cases agreement was 100%.

EXPERIMENTAL PHASES

Baseline. Before experimental manipulations, the frequency with which Jerry wore the orthodontic device was noted for an eight-day period. During this phase Jerry was not told the purpose of the observations. As depicted in Figure 1, the mean baseline rate was 25%.

Social Reinforcement. During Baseline$_1$, Mrs. T. noticed that she was giving Jerry attention, in the form of reprimands, when the bands were not in place. During the second phase of the study, Jerry's mother did not refer to the orthodontic device when her son was not wearing it, but praised him if the bands were in place when she made the five daily time sample checks. For the nine days of contingent social reinforcement, the orthodontic device was in place 36% of the time.

Delayed Monetary Payoff. Dissatisfied with Jerry's progress during Social Reinforcement, Mrs. T. explored the effectiveness of paying her son money when he was wearing the dental device. Mrs. T. told Jerry that each time he was checked and the bands were in place he would receive 25 cents. If the bands were not in place he would lose 25 cents. The results were marked on a kitchen calendar after each observation, with the exchange of money taking place at the end of the month. For the 15 days of Delayed Monetary Payoff, the mean rate of wearing the apparatus increased to 60%.

Immediate Monetary Payoff$_1$. Although the frequency of appropriate behavior increased to more than twice the Baseline$_1$ rate during Delayed Monetary Payoff, Jerry's mother attempted to achieve further gains. During the Immediate

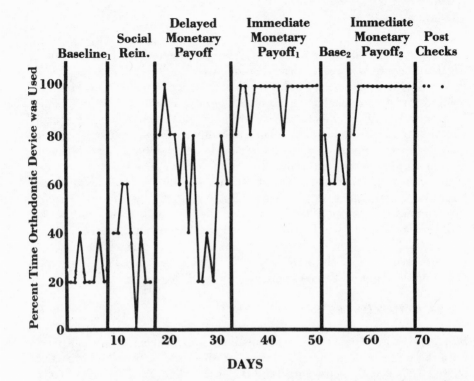

Figure 1. A record of the percentage of time a teen-age boy used an orthodontic device. Measurements were taken five times a day at varying intervals. *Baseline₁*—before experimental manipulations. *Social Reinforcement*—ignoring subject when he was not wearing the device and praising him when he was. *Delayed Monetary Payoff*—paying youngster 25 cents when he had apparatus in place during an observation, and charging him 25 cents when it was not in place. Monetary exchange took place at end of month. *Immediate Monetary Payoff₁*—same as Delayed Monetary Payoff except that money was exchanged immediately after each check. *Baseline₂*—reinstatement of Baseline₁. *Immediate Monetary Payoff₂*—reinstatement of Immediate Monetary Payoff₁. *Post Checks*—periodic checks after termination of formal experiment.

Monetary Payoff₁ phase, Mrs. T. and Jerry made the 25-cent exchange immediately after each of the five daily observations. For the 18 days of this contingency the mean rate increased to 97%.

Baseline₂. Prior to a five-day reversal phase, Mrs. T. informed Jerry that he was making excellent progress in improving his mouth structure and that monetary exchange no longer seemed necessary. The mean rate of 64% that occurred during the Baseline₂ phase was greater than the rate during Baseline₁, Social Reinforcement, and Delayed Monetary Payoff, but below that during Immediate Monetary Payoff₁.

Immediate Monetary Payoff₂. Jerry was again paid immediately for wearing the orthodontic apparatus and lost money if the device was not in place. During the 13 days of this phase, the subject was wearing the apparatus on 98.5% of the checks.

Post Checks. On Day 68, Mrs. T. informed Jerry that money would be exchanged during each observation, but that checks would be made only occasionally. On Days 70, 71, and 74 single checks were made and in each case Jerry was wearing the orthodontic device. Observations were then made at intervals approximately two weeks apart. The bands were consistently in place. Eight months after the study was initiated, the dentist indicated that great progress in Jerry's mouth structure had been achieved, and that it was no longer necessary to wear the apparatus.

EXPERIMENT 2

SUBJECT AND SETTING

For six months, Mrs. G. tried, without success, to get Antoinette, a 10-yr-old girl, to perform routine household tasks, such as cleaning her bedroom, sweeping the floor, and making her bed. Verbal reminders and unsystematic punishment produced little improvement in Antoinette's behavior.

OBSERVATIONS

Table 1 contains a list of the eight tasks and a brief definition of those tasks that Mrs. G. expected Antoinette to complete. Each day, Mrs. G. kept a record of the tasks Antoinette performed and the points she earned on a chart. During experimental phases the chart was posted on Antoinette's bedroom door. Checks were made each day just before the evening meal at about 6:00 p.m. Throughout the study, a neighbor made reliability checks every four to six days. The neighbor periodically made "visits" just before supper. She made an independent record of the points earned on a separate recording sheet and the records were then compared item by item. On several occasions, Mrs. G. made specific requests in the neighbor's presence for Antoinette to do odd jobs to check agreement on whether or not she complied. All 13 reliability checks resulted in 100% agreement.

EXPERIMENTAL PHASES

Baseline₁. As depicted in Figure 2, baseline conditions were in effect for eight days. Mrs. G. explained to Antoinette that mother was extremely busy lately and that Antoinette, being "a big girl," was expected to share the responsibility for household tasks. Mrs. G. had devised the point system for the chores at this time

Table 1
The examples of points Antoinette could earn each day for completing eight household tasks.

Task	Points
Bed made up—Covers straight, neat and smooth, sheets not visible, pillows covered, blankets folded, no other items on bed.	5
Clothes hung properly—Clothes hung straight on hangers in closet, no hangers on closet door.	5
Personal articles neatly placed—Top of dresser neat, articles arranged in symmetrical array, no powder spilled, etc.	5
Floor swept—No cement dust film on floor (Home was of cinder block construction in housing project where white powdery dust accumulated quickly).	5
Straighten and dust living room—Magazines on shelves, TV in place (not where A watched it on floor), table cleaned, books in place, no dust on furniture.	10
Kitchen duties—Wash or dry dishes, dishes in cupboard, towel on rack.	20
Bathroom duties—Towel on rack, soap in soap dish, lavatory clean and dry.	20
Odd jobs on request—Clean out car, bring in groceries, sweep off porch, etc.	5-20

but had not revealed it to Antoinette. During this period, Antoinette completed only two tasks for an average of 1.25 points per day.

Points. Mrs. G. described the point system to Antoinette. A graph was placed on the door of Antoinette's bedroom with a chart indicating the number of points that could be earned for each task. Every evening, the mother and daughter recorded the points that Antoinette earned that day. During the six days in which this contingency was in effect, Antoinette's average increased to 16.7 points per day. The range of completed tasks was from two to four a day.

Pennies. The Pennies stage of the experiment was the same as the Points stage, except that each point could be exchanged for one penny. During the nine days that this system was employed, the mean number of points increased to 36.7 with a range from 0 to 55 points.

Campfire Uniform. During the final day of the Pennies stage, Antoinette returned from school with a request form to join the Campfire Girls. Mrs. G. signed the form and told Antoinette that she could save the points she earned and exchange them for the blouse and skirt of the uniform that prospective Campfire Girls were expected to purchase. Mrs. G. assigned a cost of 400 points to each item of the uniform. By the nineteenth day of this stage, Antoinette had earned in excess of 800 points and was able to purchase the blouse and skirt. The mean number of points earned was 42.4 per day.

Baseline₂. Baseline conditions were reinstated for eight days. Mrs. G. told her daughter that she was nearing the end of the graph paper and that future reinforcement would not be available until "my next paycheck comes." The mean of 15.6 points for this period was greater than that during Baseline₁, but below the means during Points, Pennies, and Campfire Uniform phases and trending downward.

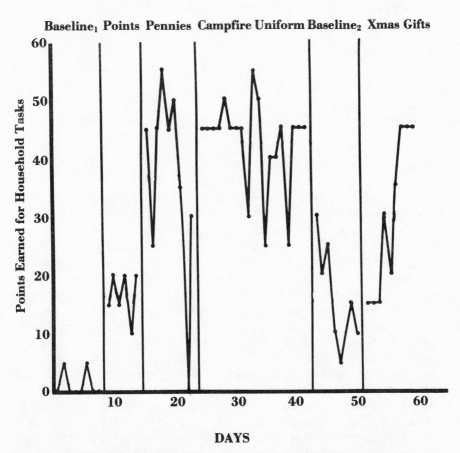

DAYS

Figure 2. The number of points a 10-yr-old girl earned each day for performing household tasks. *Baseline₁*—before experimental manipulations. *Points*—graphing the points the subject earned each day. *Pennies*—points were exchanged for pennies at the rate of one penny per point. *Campfire Uniform*—points were exchanged for blouse and skirt of campfire uniform at rate of 400 points per item. *Baseline₂*—reinstatement of Baseline₁. *Xmas Gifts*—points could be exchanged for money toward purchase of Christmas gifts, at rate of one penny per point.

Christmas Gifts. Mrs. G. informed Antoinette that the points she earned could be saved toward the purchase of Christmas gifts, at the exchange rate of one penny per point. The mean number of points for the nine days of this phase was 29.4. This average was greater than that achieved during $Baseline_1$, Points, or $Baseline_2$, but below the means attained during the Pennies and Campfire Uniform stages. It should be noted, however, that the number of points Antoinette earned was increasing and they had in fact reached the level of the previous reinforcement stage in the last four days of the Christmas Gifts phase.

EXPERIMENT 3

SUBJECT AND SETTING

The subject was a 4-yr-old boy who, according to his parents' reports, whined and shouted at a high frequency. The experiment took place in Terry's home.

OBSERVATIONS

A record of Terry's verbalizations, which were of such pitch and loudness that the observer considered them to be whines or shouts, was kept by the subject's parents. Measurements were taken from approximately 9:00 a.m. to 9:00 p.m. On weekdays, Mrs. J. kept a daily record from 9:00 a.m. until 6:00 p.m., whereas Mr. J. noted the frequency from 6:00 p.m. until 9:00 p.m. Mr. J. recorded the data from 9:00 a.m. until 9:00 p.m. on weekends. Terry went to a morning nursery for 2 hr three times a week and occasionally was left with a babysitter. No records were kept during these intervals but since they occurred during all phases of the study there was no indication the data were significantly affected. Reliability checks were attained six times by having both parents record behaviors simultaneously for the entire day.

When only one parent was recording, cries, whines, and complaints were tallied on recording sheets, one of which was posted in the kitchen, one in the parent's bedroom. On weekend days when reliability checks were made, the mother tallied on the recording sheets. The father tallied with a pencil on a piece of paper he carried in his pocket. At the end of the day the tallies were totalled. The reliability index was determined by dividing the smaller observed frequency by the larger observed frequency. Agreement ranged between 75 and 100% with a mean of 85.5%. Interestingly, the experimental extinction procedures did not seem to affect reliability measures; the mean agreement during baseline sessions was 85% while that during experimental phases was 86%.

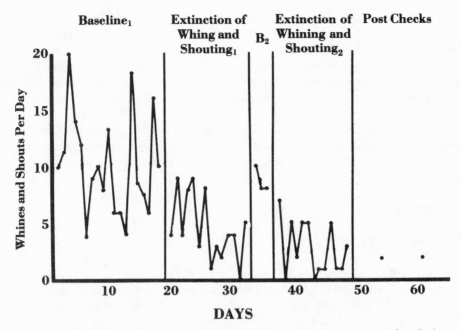

Figure 3. The frequency of shouts and screams per day made by a 4-yr-old boy. *Baseline₁*—before experimental manipulations. *Extinction of Whining and Shouting₁*—ignoring inappropriate verbalizations. *Baseline₂*—reinstatement of Baseline₁. *Extinction of Whining and Shouting₂*—reinstatement of previous extinction procedure. *Post Checks*—observations of subject after formal termination of experiment.

EXPERIMENTAL PHASES

Baseline₁. The frequency of Terry's shouts and whines under "normal" conditions was recorded for 19 days. During this period, mother and father attended to their son's inappropriate verbalizations by either comforting him or ordering him to stop. Figure 3 indicates that the mean number of whines and shouts for the baseline period was 10.2 per day.

Extinction of Whining and Shouting₁. During the second phase of the study, Terry's parents ignored him when he whined or shouted. If he emitted an inappropriate verbalization, mother and father turned away from him and engaged in other activities. Whenever possible, they left the area entirely. For the 14 days of extinction, the mean number of whines and shouts decreased to 4.6 per day. The consistency of the effect was demonstrated by the fact that all 14 data points during this period were below the mean that occurred during Baseline₁.

Baseline₂. Baseline conditions were reinstated for three days. Mr. and Mrs. J. again attended to Terry when he whined or shouted. The mean for this phase increased to 8.7 verbalizations per day.

Extinction of Whining and Shouting₂. For 13 days, Terry's parents again ignored his inappropriate verbal behaviors. The mean number of whines and shouts decreased to 2.8 per day. This average was below that attained during the previous extinction stage.

Post Checks. On the fifth and eleventh days of the experiment after the formal termination of Extinction of Whining and Shouting₂, post checks on Terry's behavior were made. During both days, a total of two whines and shouts was noted.

EXPERIMENT 4

SUBJECT AND SETTING

Elaise, a 5-year-old preschool girl, had a tendency to take long periods of time to dress herself after waking each morning. Her mother's efforts in putting the clothes out the previous night and insisting that she get dressed more quickly were ineffective in changing Elaise's behavior.

OBSERVATIONS

Mrs. R. consulted her wrist watch and recorded on a chart the time to the nearest minute that Elaise arose and the time at which she became fully dressed. Arising meant leaving her bed by placing both feet on the floor to begin her daily activities after being called by her mother each morning. Fully dressed meant being clothed in the shoes, stockings, underclothes, dress/or play clothes the mother had laid out for Elaise the night before. Reliability checks were made on four occasions by an 8-yr-old sister and on one occasion by Elaise's aunt who was visiting in the home. Mrs. R. synchronized her watch with the kitchen clock used by the second observers. The sister gave a verbal report to Mrs. R. indicating the times when Elaise arose and finished dressing. The aunt made an independent written record. All five checks resulted in 100% agreement.

EXPERIMENTAL PHASES

Baseline₁. A record of the amount of time Elaise spent in dressing during all experimental sessions is shown in Figure 4. Under "normal" conditions, the range of times was from 1 hr 0 min to 6 hr 35 min. The mean rate for the 18 days of Baseline₁ was 3 hr 10 min.

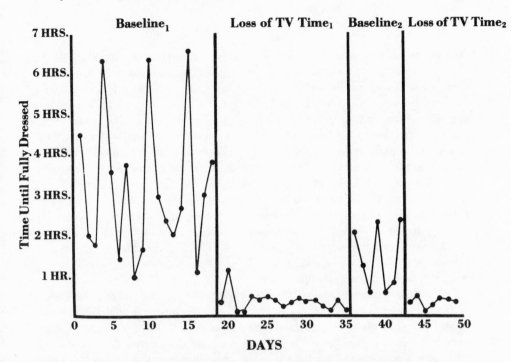

Figure 4. Duration of time it took a 5-yr-old girl to get dressed after waking. *Baseline₁*—before experimental procedures. *Loss of TV Time₁*—subject was not permitted to watch television if she was not dressed within 30 min of arising. *Baseline₂*—reinstatment of Baseline₁. *Loss of TV Time₂*—reinstatement of Loss of TV Time₁.

Loss of TV Time₁. Beginning with Day 19, Elaise was required to finish dressing within 30 min after awaking. If she failed to meet the criterion, she was not permitted to watch television until 3:30 p.m. that day. During the 17 days this contingency was in effect, her average dressing time was 23 min. Only once did she miss her television privileges.

Baseline₂. The punishment criterion was removed for seven days. The mean duration of dressing time during this phase was 1 hr 26 min. This rate was greater than that occuring during the Loss of TV Time₁ stage but lower than the rate during Baseline₁.

Loss of TV Time₂. Elaise was again required to dress within 30 min after waking. Her mean dressing time for the seven days of this condition was 20 min. This average was 3 min less than the average during loss of TV Time₁.

DISCUSSION

One of the most frequently stated advantages of operant conditioning techniques is that the procedures are uncomplicated and can easily be applied in therapeutic situations. Nevertheless, a perusal of the pertinent literature indicates the presence of relatively few investigators of operant principles. One hypothesis for this finding might be that although the application of operant conditioning principles is simple, scientific investigation remains a complex task. The above studies, like those reported by Hall, Axelrod, Foundopoulos, Shellman, Campbell, and Cranston (1971) and Hall, Fox, Willard, Goldsmith, Emerson, Owen, Porcia, and Davis (1971) indicated, however, that individuals with relatively little training in operant techniques can devise and conduct behavioral experiments without unduly compromising scientific rigor. In each experiment, the investigator provided procedural manipulations (*i.e.*, a "reversal" design) that strengthened the validity of his findings. The experimenter served as the primary observer for his study, but also used a second observer to establish the reliability of his measurements.

The problem behaviors in the above experiments are typical of those found in many homes. The difficulties were not sufficiently severe that the parents sought clinical assistance, but they were a source of family friction and could have led to greater problems if a solution were not discovered. An example of this notion was given in Experiment I. The orthodontist indicated that had Jerry used the dental device when treatments were first started, his mouth structure would have been corrected in less than a year, and his parents could have saved approximately $2100 in dental fees. The cost of the experiment was less than $30.

In Experiments I and II, different positive reinforcement techniques, including token and social reinforcement, increased the frequency of appropriate behaviors. In Experiment III, an extinction procedure resulted in a decrease in whining and shouting, and in Experiment IV, contingent punishment eliminated the excessive dressing time of a 5-yr-old girl. The studies were designed in such a manner that the experimenter (*i.e.*, parent) could apply the procedures and record the data without significantly upsetting his daily routine. This factor is crucial for studies conducted in a home environment because the investigator usually cannot devote his entire attention to the problem behavior. The fact that the investigators were able to employ resources that are already found in most homes increases the general applicability of the present experiments.

A frequent criticism of behavior modification studies is that although the subject often demonstrates a dramatic change in behavior, the procedures are applied for a relatively short period of time. In Experiment I, however, the study was continued for eight months, at which time the problem situation was completely corrected. The procedures in Experiment II were still being applied at the time this article was written, approximately 2 yr and a move to Texas after the home token system was originally instituted, although the original techniques were modified somewhat. Mrs. G. reported that the tasks required for reinforcement had changed and that Antoinette now helped choose the back-up reinforcers. When Mrs. G. had suggested they discontinue the procedures Antoinette had stated: "Mommy, I can just do a better job when I can see how I'm doing." Apparently the effects of the procedure favorably impressed others in the subject's environment. Mrs. G. reported that an older daughter observed the change in Antoinette's behavior, read several operant conditioning studies, and subsequently trained the family cat to sit up, shake hands, and roll over. In addition, a neighbor of Mrs. G., who originally performed reliability checks, reported success with similar behavior modification techniques with her six children. The implications are obvious if effective systems are being developed that can be adapted and put to practical use without the requirement for formal study or training.

The procedures for recording and for obtaining checks on the reliability of observations in these studies were devised by the parents who carried them out.

In three studies, 100% agreement was obtained and in the third experiment, an acceptable level (85.5%) was achieved. The high reliability of observation may have been influenced by several factors. One factor may have been that the behaviors chosen were for the most part rather discrete and easily discriminated. In the first experiment, the parents agreed that it was easy to see whether or not the bands were in place. They either were or they were not. Mrs. G. stated that it was easy to make a similar decision about whether or not tasks were completed in Experiment II. They either were or were not done. One thing that helped to make this so was the great amount of fine white dust present in the housing project where they lived, which aided in discriminating as to whether sweeping and dusting had occurred. During the experimental phases, Antoinette participated in marking the chart, which was a further check on the accuracy of recording. In Experiment IV, Mrs. R. reported there was little trouble in knowing when Elaise had arisen for she arose quickly after being called and had to leave her bed either to get her clothes, which had been laid out, or to come to breakfast, watch television, or engage in other high-probability behaviors. It was also easy to see when she was fully dressed. During experimental phases, Elaise promptly informed her mother when she was dressed because to do so was in her own best interest. This, of course, assisted her mother in noting the time promptly during these phases. In Experiment III, it was perhaps less easy to make such a discrimination. For one thing, the behavior was auditorally perceived rather than visually, tone and inflection were involved and event recording or a frequency count of transient events was involved, rather than direct measurement of a permanent product (See Hall, 1971) as was the case in the other three studies. These differences may have accounted for the somewhat lower, yet acceptable agreement found in Experiment III.

Another factor may have been related to the fact that the independence of the observers is somewhat open to question. Azrin, Holz, Ulrich, and Goldiamond (1961) pointed out the importance of independent reliability checks. In Experiment I, Mr. T. made a verbal report of his observation decision to Mrs. T. which she recorded after having recorded her own "+" or "0". It would have been "cleaner" had he made an independent simultaneous record in which he recorded "+" or "0" on his own sheet with the records being compared at the end of the day's observation. Nevertheless, the method used was an approximation, was pragmatic, and was better than no reliability check. In Experiment II, a more rigorous and acceptably independent procedure was used. In Experiment III, a good attempt at independent recording was made, although the records could have been affected by the fact that it may have been possible for one or the other of the parents to see when cries, whines, or complaints were being recorded or, during experimental phases, when extinction procedures were being carried out. The latter case would not seem to have been true, however, since similar percentages of agreement were found during the baseline and extinction phases.

In Experiment IV, a problem similar to that noted in Experiment I was evident. In this case, the age of the sibling who acted as a second observer may have influenced the parent to alter the recording procedure the sister used. In other instances, however, young observers have proven to be reliable observers and recorders of behavior (Hall, Cristler, Cranston, and Tucker, 1970). The fact that an aunt did carry out one entirely independent check using a similar recording technique does lend credence to the observational record.

Another factor common to all the studies is that in each case the primary observer was aware that a reliability check was in progress. Romanczyk, Kent, Diament, and O'Leary (1971) provided some evidence that agreement improves when the primary observer is aware that a check is being made, even though the difference in agreement may not be significant.

Some deficiencies have been pointed out in the rigor with which the observation and reliability procedures were carried out in these studies. It should be emphasized, however, that at the time they were conducted some 2 to 3 yr ago they compared favorably along these dimensions with many studies carried out in more controlled settings.

Subsequent studies carried out by parents who have participated in the Responsive Teaching course have become increasingly sophisticated and rigorous along these dimensions. The long lead time between writing up, submitting, reviewing, revising, and publishing, however, means that by the time more sophisticated studies are published they too will be outdated. We would like to mention, however, that currently, whenever possible, in addition to the reliability checks carried out by the *"in vivo"* second observers, at least one additional check is carried out by the group leader of the Responsive Teaching class. It has been noted in our experience that high levels of agreement between observers and similar levels of behavior to those being reported have been consistently found.

Perhaps it would be well to note another kind of reliability as to the efficacy of the studies and of the procedures used, which was first pointed out by Amber Tribble (1968). Mrs. Tribble carried out a study in which she attempted to lose weight by decreasing her calorie intake. At the end of the study she pointed out that the decrease in the number of calories would, according to health authorities, result in the approximate weight loss she actually obtained. In Experiment I, a similar kind of validation occurred when Jerry's dentist, R. D. Boice, D.D.S., stated that Jerry's mouth structure had suddenly begun to improve once experimental procedures were begun and that by his estimate the parents could have saved several years and $2100 had they employed them 8 yr earlier. By the same token, in Experiment II, the fact that Mrs. G.'s neighbor, Mrs. Frances McGuire, deciced to use the procedures with her own children is an indication at least that they were being carried out and were effective.

It is of further interest perhaps to note that both Mrs. G. and Mr. and Mrs. T. are continuing to use token reinforcement procedures to maintain appropriate behavior in their offspring over 2 yr after completion of their studies, even though the behaviors worked with have changed. In the other two cases, the original behaviors are no longer reported to be problems and similar procedures have not been systematically used, although Terry's parents report that they have been careful to use their attention to reinforce appropriate behavior, albeit unsystematically.

REFERENCES

Azrin, N. H., Holz, W. H., Ulrich, R., and Goldiamond, I. Control of the content of conversation through reinforcement. *Journal of the Experimental Analysis of Behavior*, 1961, **4,** 25-30.

Hall, R. V. Behavior Management Series. *Part I. The Measurement of Behavior, Part II. Basic Principles, Part III. Applications in School and Home.* H and H Enterprises, 1971.

Hall, R. V., Axelrod, S., Foundopoulos, M., Shellman, J., Campbell, R. A., and Cranston, S. S. The effective use of punishment in the classroom. *Educational Technology*, 1971, Vol. XI, **4,** 24-26.

Hall, R. V. and Copeland, R. E. *The responsive teaching model: A first step in shaping school personnel as behavior modification specialists.* A paper presented at the Third Banff International Conference on Behavior Modification, April, 1971.

Hall, R. V., Cristler, C., Cranston, S. S., and Tucker, B. Teachers and parents as researchers using multiple baseline designs. *Journal of Applied Behavior Analysis*, 1970, **3**, 247-255.

Hall, R. V., Fox, R., Willard, D., Goldsmith, L., Emerson, M., Owen, M., Davis, F., and Porcia, E. The teacher as observer and experimenter in the modification of disputing and talking-out behaviors. *Journal of Applied Behavior Analysis*, 1971, **4**, 141-149.

Hawkins, R. P., Peterson, R. F., Schweid, D., and Bijou, S. W. Behavior therapy in the home: Amelioration of problem parent-child relations with the parent in a therapeutic role. *Journal of Experimental Child Psychology*, **4**, 99-107.

Romanczyk, R. G., Kent, R. N., Diament, C., and O'Leary, K. D. *Methodological problems in naturalistic observation*. Paper presented at the Second Kansas Follow Through Symposium on Applied Behavior Analysis, April, 1971.

Tribble, A. *Reduction of caloric intake through a self-imposed consequence*. Unpublished study, Education 115, University of Kansas, 1968.

Wahler, R. G. Oppositional children: a quest for parental reinforcement control. *Journal of Applied Behavior Analysis*, 1969, **2**, 159-170.

Zeilberger, J., Sampen, S. E., and Sloane, H. N. Modification of a child's problem behaviors in the home with the mother as therapist. *Journal of Applied Behavior Analysis*, 1968, **1**, 47-53.

Chapter 11

Systematic Observation and Reinforcement Technique in Toilet Training[1]
Donald K. Pumroy and Shirley S. Pumroy

Summary.—At 26 and 29 mo. of age the authors' son and daughter were rewarded with an after dinner mint for asking to be allowed to urinate and completing the act successfully. The male was observed until he was 30 mo. and the female until she was 34 mo. Learning was observed in each child. No emotional problems appeared.

It is obvious to any student of the American culture that toilet training of children receives a great deal of attention. Not only is toilet training an area of concern to mothers, as judged by the amount of space devoted to this subject in newspapers, magazines, and how-to-raise children books, but it is also viewed as important by personality theorists and much space in textbooks is devoted to this topic. It is therefore difficult to understand why there has been almost no research on toilet training *per se*. What research has been done has typically consisted of using two groups of Ss, one toilet-trained by one method and another group trained differently, to evaluate personality differences between groups. How and when Ss were toilet trained was usually stated by Ss' mothers. The problems involved in retrospective data, particularly reliability, have been pointed out by Wenar (1961). The authors are aware of only one study (McGraw, 1940) that actually investigated the learning process in toilet training. This study does not include the later stage of learning in which the child takes the responsibility for going to the toilet.

[1]Reprinted with permission from *Psychological Reports* 16 (1965): 467-71.

There are several possible reasons for the lack of research in toilet training. One might be that this is often viewed as a taboo area. Another reason may be that data collection on children of this age is difficult in that they are not conveniently grouped for research as they are in nursery school. This is a period when the child is in the home with the parents and thus it is necessary to study one at a time. Another deterrent to research in this area may be the large amount of time involved in studying the toilet-training-learning process. Despite these problems, such a study was undertaken, to provide data on toilet training (urination only) for two children, a male and a female.

METHOD

SUBJECTS

Ss were children of the authors. Both children were healthy, normal, and bowel trained at the start of the study. As it has been recommended (Brazelton, 1962) that urine training begin around 2 yr., training was not started before that time. There was some delay with the female because of illness in the family. The male was 26 mo. and the female 29 mo. at the beginning of the learning period, and they were 30 mo. and 34 mo., respectively, at the end.

PROCEDURE

The male child, being the elder, was first studied. Initially he did not ask to go to the toilet. As he was successful in urinating in the toilet, he was taken to the toilet at various times during the day, i.e., upon arising, before going to bed, before going out, etc. This procedure continued throughout the study. At the beginning he frequently wet his pants even though he was taken to the toilet. On Day 1 the number of times he wet his pants was recorded. This was repeated on Day 2. On the morning of Day 3 the child was called to the bathroom. He urinated and was given a small after dinner mint. These small after dinner mints were used because they were liked and because they dissolved rapidly. By dissolving rapidly it was felt that the mints would be most likely to reinforce the immediately preceding sequence of behavior. A reward such as a lollipop would have been less effective. He was told that whenever he asked to go to the toilet and did he would be given a mint. If he asked to go to the toilet and was unable to urinate he was not allowed to stay on the toilet more than 5 min. Each time he was given a mint it was recorded. Also recorded was each time that he wet his pants.

The female child was treated in a similar manner except that the number of times wet was recorded for 2 weeks before the reward was introduced. Data were collected for 168 days.

RESULTS

The data collected for the male child are presented in Fig. 1. This shows the number of times wet and the number of times the child asked to go to the toilet and did.

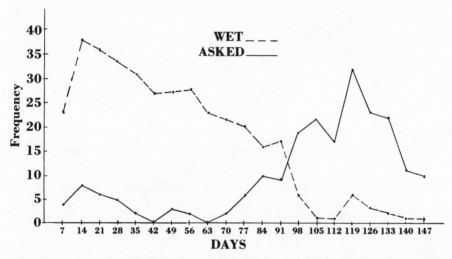

Figure 1. Number of times male child asked to go to the toilet and number of times he was wet in seven-day blocks

Two figures are presented for the data collected for the female child. Fig. 2 was prepared to show the effect of reinforcement on her requests to go to the toilet. Fig. 2 shows the number of times she asked during a period of 5 days before the mint was introduced and 5 days after. She had learned to ask to go to the toilet to some extent from her older brother. It was in the afternoon of Day 6 that the reward was introduced so Day 6 is plotted twice, once before the reward was introduced and then after. Fig. 3 presents the over-all learning curve and is similar to Fig. 1 for the male.

DISCUSSION AND CONCLUSIONS

The curve for the male child indicates that learning did take place. Note that the "times wet" curve rises and stays high on the first part of the curve. This may be due to negative behavior, i.e., "getting back at" *E* for not giving him a mint at times other than when he went to the toilet. Also, it may have been that he felt that urination was being rewarded but had not differentiated between the parts of the behavioral chain and that to obtain reward he had to urinate in the toilet.

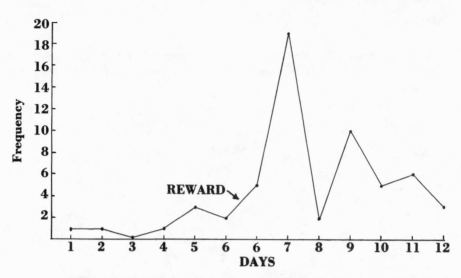

Figure 2. Number of times female child asked to go to the toilet

It is also of interest to note the rise in the "times asked" curve once the asking was mastered and then the decline. This may be due to the fact that the

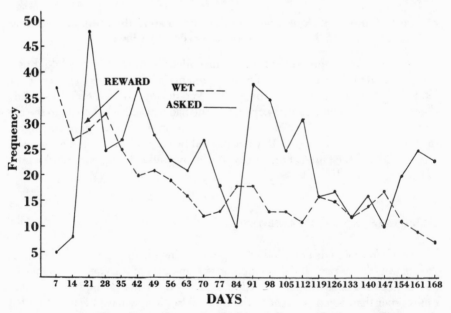

Figure 3. Number of times female child asked to go to toilet and number of times she was wet in seven-day block

novelty of the reward wore off or because of advancing neuromuscular development retention of urine for longer periods was possible.

The change in response determined from comparison of the 5 days before reinforcement and the 5 days after reinforcement suggests that the introduction of the reward did have an effect for the female child. The over-all data indicate that learning did take place. At the end of the study she was wet only on rising in the morning.

The shapes of the times-asked curves for the two children are quite different, while the wet curves are more similar. Note that for the female the times-asked curve rises as soon as the mint is introduced and roughly parallels the times wet curve. It seems from this that during most of the time studied, she was more able to control her sphincter than was the male. Perhaps this related to the fact that the female was 3 mo. older than the male was when they were first studied. Also note that, while the female had more control than the male at the start, the male had better control at the end of their learning curve. This was primarily due to the female's being wet in the morning while the male was not.

While the authors and others have had some qualms about the possible emotional effect from this study on the children's later toilet habits and personalities, no problems have been noted. For both children the end of the study coincided with a vacation, during which the mints were not available nor were they available after the vacation. By that time the children were toilet trained and did not mention the mints.

This study raises some interesting and provocative questions. When parents are asked at what age was their child toilet trained, how and to what are they responding? Considering the curves presented here, is the child toilet trained when the curves cross? When the "times asked" curve exceeds the "times wet" curve for a certain number of days? Or when the "times wet" curve falls to zero? What are the effects of the other techniques of toilet training? How are these manifested in learning curves? Are sex differences in toilet training similar to those presented? Could training be started earlier with the same results? Several lines of research seem obvious.

In conclusion, this study shows (1) toilet training does take place with this reinforcement technique, (2) this technique does not appear to cause any emotional problems and (3) systematic observation of toilet training is useful for various comparative purposes.

REFERENCES

Brazelton, T. B. A child-oriented approach to toilet training. *Pediat.*, 1962, 29, 121-128.

McGraw, M. B. Neural maturation as exemplified in achievement of bladder control. *Pediat.*, 1940, 16, 580-590.

Wenar, C. The reliability of mothers' histories. *Child Developm.*, 1961, 32, 491-500.

Chapter 12

The Application of Operant Conditioning in Toilet Training[1]

Marilyn Miller Schwartz

During the writer's last semester of college, she was asked by her brother and sister-in-law for advice in toilet-training their three-and-a-half-year-old daughter. Since the child, as judged by the family pediatrician, was physically capable of being toilet trained, the writer agreed to work with the parents in training the child. At first, the writer's advice consisted of a series of candid pseudoscientific suggestions. However, when it became apparent that such advice had little or no effect on the child's behavior, it was decided by the writer that an organized plan of action, based on sound principles, should be initiated. Consequently, the writer obtained a guarantee of complete cooperation from the parents and began the construction of such a plan based upon principles of operant conditioning.

To begin with, the writer set out to define the dynamic aspects of the situation. After initial observations, it was decided that the behavioral problem was twofold. First of all, the base level of the desirable behavior of eliminating on the toilet was clearly zero and second, an undesirable and conflicting behavior— of the child eliminating in her diapers—was occurring quite consistently and being reinforced by the parents. To give the reader a feeling for this problem, included below is an early conversation held between the child's mother, Linda, and the writer.

[1]Unpublished honors research, University of Maryland, College Park, Md.

WRITER: *But, Linda, you explained to me that Karen (the child in this study) won't defecate or urinate on the toilet, so where and when does she eliminate?*

MOTHER: *Karen refuses to use the toilet, so I diaper her before she is put to bed at night and before her daily nap. When I wake her up in the mornings and after her nap, she usually has her pants full.*

WRITER: *But, what happens if Karen misses her nap, will she make in her pants?*

MOTHER: *No, only once or twice that I can remember did she ever make in her pants and at the time, she was severely scolded. Usually, what she does is to literally "hold it in" until she becomes very constipated.*

WRITER: *Doesn't she mind this?*

MOTHER: *I think she must because she often becomes extremely irritable when she misses her nap or when the family stays out late and she doesn't have a chance to relieve herself. She often nags me when we're out, saying, "Mommy, I want to go home and go to bed."*

WRITER: *Doesn't it annoy her to wear wet and dirty diapers?*

MOTHER: *No, I really don't think so. In fact, she is very cheerful when I pick her up after her nap and in the mornings when I change and bathe her.*

WRITER: *How many times a day do you bathe her?*

MOTHER: *Because of her diaper-wetting and the threat of diaper rash, I often bathe her twice a day.*

WRITER: *Is she talkative then?*

MOTHER: *Extremely. In fact, she can be her sweetest self at bathing time, especially, since she isn't fighting with her [older—5½-year-old] sister.*

WRITER: *Have you discussed toilet training with Karen at all?*

MOTHER: *Practically all of the time. In fact, it is the most discussed topic around our house. Now that Karen is in nursery school, it's really important that she use the toilet. Imagine, her nursery school teacher called last week and asked if there was any particular reason why Karen refuses to enter the bathroom with the rest of the children, when they are taken in there at noon. Because only toilet-trained children are allowed to go to this private school, I didn't explain her problem to the teacher, especially since Karen has never had an accident at school.*

WRITER: *Do you discuss this matter with your husband in front of the children?*

MOTHER: *Yes, Howard and I discuss this matter often in front of the children. In fact, we often argue over it. Howard gets mad and says Karen is nothing but a baby and we should just take away her diapers and not put them on her at nap-time and at night.*

WRITER: *Have you ever tried this?*

MOTHER: *Not exactly. But, I often tried waking Karen up earlier than usual and then taking off her diapers before she had time to go in them. I felt that out of necessity, she might use the toilet. However, she would again just "hold it in" and I would be stuck with a constipated and irritable child on my hands. As a result, I usually now do the opposite by waking her up and giving her a few minutes to play in her crib and wet her pants.*

Although the above represents only one of the many conversations held between the mother and the writer, it does give the reader a good feeling for the problem. Reviewing what was said, the mother did answer that the child never used the toilet for urinating or defecating. Also, the mother stated that the frequency of the child's behavior of wetting her diapers was fairly high, in fact, it appeared to be a highly consistent and predictable behavior.

Defining "eliminating on the toilet" as the desirable behavior and "wetting the diapers" as the undesirable behavior, the writer then analyzed the situation to determine why the response strength of the latter undesirable behavior was so much higher and how the situation could be reversed. In a close examination of the above conversation, certain possibilities are revealed.

First of all, from the mother's statements, it is apparent that the child was receiving a great deal of reinforcement for the undesirable behavior. Besides her mother's twice-a-day pamperings, there were frequent conversations between the parents about toilet training, focusing additional attention on the child. Also, as evidence for the reinforcing consequences of diaper-wetting, the child often expressed pleasure during her diaperings and changings and, according to her mother's verbal report, she didn't seem to show any signs of displeasure with the discomforts of wet diapers. Also, the fact that the child would voluntarily constipate herself in order to continue this undesirable behavior, is some indication of the strength of the behavior itself and the reinforcing consequences that sustained it. As far as the reason for the infrequent (or actually zero) occurrence of the desirable behavior, the evidence is less obvious. However, the fact that the undesirable behavior of wetting the diapers physically conflicts with the desirable behavior of eliminating on the toilet explains why reinforcing of one behavior (in this case, the undesirable behavior of diaper-wetting) would increase the response strength of that behavior and would make it highly improbable that the other, conflicting behavior (of eliminating on the toilet) would occur.

Applying the principles of operant conditioning, the writer concluded that the best way to reverse the response strengths of the two conflicting behaviors was to reverse the nature of their consequences. In other words, a plan was constructed in which reinforcement would be given only after the occurrence of the desirable behavior. Hopefully, it was expected that in doing so, the response strength of the desirable behavior would increase and the response strength of the undesirable behavior would decrease and eventually would extinguish. To show the general direction that the toilet-training was to take, included below is a copy of the set of directions sent to the mother. (These directions were included in a letter sent to the mother. The beginning of this letter, containing an explanation of the principles of operant conditioning, has been omitted.)

Linda, please try to follow these directions as closely as possible. If you have any questions, please call me.

WEEK 1—*Post the data sheet on the bathroom door and record each time Karen urinates, or defecates, or both. Just check under the correct columns. Please try to keep an accurate account even though this chore may become annoying.*

WEEK 2—*Please refrain from giving Karen any candy. You can let Jane have some. Keep up with the data recording. Also, stop discussing anything about toilet-training with your husband when the child is in hearing distance. Also, do not pamper Karen during the mornings or afternoons, when you change her diapers and clean her up. Try to limit your conversations with her at this time and pay her as little attention as possible.*

WEEK 3—*Continue to record the data, don't discuss toilet training in front of the child, and be placid while diapering and changing her. Also, begin bringing Karen into the bathroom immediately before putting her to bed and shortly after she has awakened. Perhaps, waking her a little earlier than usual and bringing her into the bathroom before she has wet her pants will make her more conducive to the toilet-training. Make sure that you bring a package of candy into the bathroom each time the child is brought in and inform her that if she uses the toilet, she will be rewarded with it. If she does eliminate on the toilet, immediately give her the package of candy and verbally praise her. If she doesn't use the toilet, be sure not to scold her or to give her any sizable amount of attention.*

WEEK 4—*Continue to follow the same instructions as for Week 3. Be sure to continue recording the data.*

WEEK 5—*Continue to follow the same instructions. However, if it appears that the frequency of diaper-wetting has considerably diminished, do not diaper Karen before her nap.*

WEEK 6—*Continue to follow the same instructions as for the previous week. However, if it appears that the undesirable behavior of diaper-wetting has been extinguished (that is, frequency of response is zero), do not diaper Karen before her nap or at night time. In case she does*

> *accidentally wet her bed, do not reprimand her. Also, begin taper-*
> *ing off on the candy and giving her more and more verbal reinforce-*
> *ments, immediately following her using the toilet and during the*
> *day, (e.g. "Karen is a big girl now; she uses the toilet.").*

WEEK 7—*Continue data keeping. If all goes according to the plan, Karen*
> *should be completely toilet-trained and verbal reinforcement*
> *should sustain the desirable behavior.*

WEEK 8—*Please send all data to me.*

Without reiterating the above instructions, they served the following purposes each week:

Week 1—to determine the base levels or operant levels of the desirable and un-desirable bits of behavior.

Week 2—to insure the effectiveness of candy as a reinforcer by placing the child in a state of deprivation; to remove all reinforcement following the occurrence of the undesirable behavior of diaper-wetting.

Week 3—to apply reinforcement immediately following the occurrence of the desirable behavior and to eliminate reinforcement after the undesirable behavior.

Week 4 through Week 8—to continue reinforcing the desirable behavior and not reinforcing the undesirable behavior.

Unfortunately, the above plan of action, with its steps and objectives out-lined, did not have very satisfying results. It was observed by the writer, at the be-ginning of the third week of training, that when the child was brought into the bathroom, she would not under any circumstances sit on the toilet. At first, the writer considered the child's protests and crying tantrums to be of an attention-getting nature and requested that the mother proceed according to the plan and ignore these outbursts. However, when it was learned several days later that these outbursts were still continuing (although no reinforcement was being given to them), the writer again closely examined the situation.

It was not until after considerable inquiry into the circumstances of the child's outbursts that the following was learned. At the time the mother first be-gan toilet-training the child, the family had just moved into a new home and was having a considerable amount of trouble with their plumbing. During this time, the toilet would often overflow while the child was sitting on it and similar out-bursts of screaming and crying would occur. Finally, after several such inci-dents, the child refused to sit on the toilet and the parents decided to discontinue toilet training until the plumbing was fixed. Once again, wetting diapers was considered an acceptable behavior by the parents and no attempt was made to place the child on the toilet. It was not until after several months had passed that a new plumbing system was installed and the parents decided to resume toilet training. However, at this time the child would not even go near the toilet and after several months of little success in toilet training, the parents contacted the writer.

Because of the above information, a new aspect of the situation was revealed. Not only was the response strength of a desirable behavior low because a conflicting and undesirable behavior was being reinforced, but also because there were reinforcing consequences for *not* performing the desirable behavior. The child had learned during her experiences with the overflowing toilet that *not* sitting on the toilet would avoid such a stimulus event as the toilet overflowing. In other words, the overflowing toilet acted as a negative reinforcer; it increased the strength of the child's response *not* to sit on the toilet, which avoided this stimulus event.

With these further elements of the situation defined, the writer began again to construct a plan of action. As in the original plan, it was considered essential that reinforcement should not be given after the occurence of the undesirable behavior. In fact, the mother even stopped bathing the child twice a day and after the nap, she only wiped the child with a cold wet rag. As previously instructed, she acted placid and cool and avoided as much physical contact with the child as possible while diapering her. What was novel about the second plan of action was a method added to overcome the negative reinforcing function of the toilet seat. True, the toilet had been fixed and its overflowing had ceased. However, it was recognized by the writer that such a discriminative stimulus (or cue) as the toilet seat could, in close association with the event of the toilet overflowing, acquire a reinforcing function. That is, even when the toilet was fixed, the toilet seat acted as a discriminative stimulus for fear, and it sustained and strengthened the tendency of not sitting on the toilet seat.

In order to avoid further emotional outbursts from the child, it was decided that the child should not be coerced into sitting on the toilet seat. Also, there would be no attempt to lure the child onto the toilet with candy, thereby placing her in a conflict-type of situation (for example, she would have to choose between the positive reinforcer, candy, and the negative reinforcer, the toilet seat and possibly the event of the toilet overflowing). Instead, it was decided that the child should be gradually conditioned to sitting on a different toilet, one which she had never had any negative experience with.

Fortunately, a new wing had recently been built onto the house and a second bathroom was available for this experiment. Because the child had had no previous experiences in this room, it was hoped that there would be little generalization to it of the negative reinforcing function of the once broken toilet.

It was decided that such a method as "shaping" would be used in order to get the desired response to occur. By reinforcing responses that more and more closely approximate the desired response, the writer hoped to increase the probability that the desired response would occur. Included below is a second set of instructions sent to the mother, which shows how the shaping process was to take place.

Included below is a set of instructions. Again I would like you to follow them exactly and continue to record your data. Remember, we have decided that instead of candy, you will use verbal reinforcement. That is, whenever the child performs the required bit of behavior, you are to immediately reward her by saying something in reference to the fact that she is "a big girl now." When Karen finally performs the desired behavior of eliminating on the toilet, you may reward her by giving her a new dress. But, remember, if it is to work as effectively as the verbal reinforcement, it must immediately follow the desired behavior. These instructions are to be considered a replacement for the original set of instructions from the fourth week on. Try to follow these directions as closely as possible.

WEEK 4—*Bring Karen into the second bathroom immediately before she goes to bed at night and before her nap. Explain to her that she is "a big girl now" and can have her own bathroom. Let her wash her teeth and her hands in the bathroom and reinforce her verbally after she has performed these tasks. Bring Karen again into the bathroom immediately after her nap and after she awakens in the morning. Repeat the process of having her wash herself in the bathroom and praise her after she has accomplished these same acts.*

WEEK 5—*When you bring Karen into the bathroom, let her wear her pajama bottoms or underpants and let her sit with the top down on the toilet. Keep her relaxed at this time by combing her hair and showing her special attention. Be sure to praise her while sitting on the toilet and let her know that she is acting like a "big girl" by sitting on the toilet.*

WEEK 6—*Continue to place Karen on the toilet with the top down, but remove her pants or her pajama bottoms before doing so. Continue to keep her occupied while sitting on the toilet and praise her frequently.*

WEEK 7—*Place Karen on the toilet seat with the top up and her pants or pajama bottoms removed. Continue to keep her occupied and verbally reinforce her for performing the desired behavior. Try to increase the length of the time that she will sit on the toilet seat.*

WEEK 8—*Give Karen as much fluids as she can stand to drink. Try to wake her a little earlier than usual from her sleep and immediately bring her into the bathroom. Let her know that all "big girls" use the bathroom before going to bed and immediately after awakening. If possible, show her how you or her sister follow such a schedule. Be sure to continue reinforcing the child for sitting on the toilet.*

WEEK 9—*Continue to do the same as last week. If Karen eliminates on the toilet, immediately reward her with the new dress and verbal praise. Be sure to refer to the fact that she is "a big girl now."*

In frequent conversations with the mother, the writer clarified many of the mother's questions and received some satisfaction that the above directions were being followed. Unfortunately, the mother did not faithfully record the information requested and what data could be salvaged is included in the results below.

RESULTS

At the end of the ninth week of the training procedure, the child finally performed the desired behavior of eliminating on the toilet. According to the mother's report, the child had become very relaxed about sitting on the toilet and one morning, without any prompting, had begun to urinate. Immediately, the child was rewarded with a new dress and the mother (out of genuine delight) verbally reinforced her for this behavior. The rest of the family was told about the child's use of the toilet and she remained the focus of attention for the remainder of the day.

TABLE 1 FREQUENCY OF DEFECATION AND URINATION
IN DIAPERS AND IN THE TOILET

| | IN DIAPER | | IN TOILET | |
WEEK	DEFECATE	URINATE	DEFECATE	URINATE
1	12	13		
2	11	13		
3	10	13		
4	9	13		
5	11	12		
6	10	13		
7	(data not available)			
8	11	14		
9	8	11		2
10	4	7	3	8
11	1	3	8	15
12	0	0	9	18

As indicated on the data sheet (included above), it took approximately one and a half weeks for the desired behavior to become consistent. At this time, the diapers were no longer put on the child. Also, to further reward the child for being a "big girl," the parents did the following things: (1) the child was given a new single bed and her room and bathroom were redecorated; (2) the child's crib and diapers were given in a ceremonial manner to a younger cousin; and

(3) the child was allowed to go shopping with her mother and pick out her own dresses for school. By the twelfth week of training, the parents were fully satisfied with the results of this toilet-training procedure. Only once after this time did the child actually wet her bed. However, on this occasion the child was not reprimanded and the incident was lightly passed over.

It is interesting to note that the parents, also, reported a change after the eleventh week of training in the general behavior of the child. According to them, the child enjoyed being praised for being a "big girl" and would perform other tasks around the house in order to earn such verbal reinforcement. Also, the child acted more pleasant in such situations as when she was unable to nap or when the family would stay out late at night.

Chapter 13

Using Parents as Contingency Managers[1]
James M. Johnson

Summary.—Parents were instructed how to eliminate the disturbing behaviors of their 2 children during the dinner meal. Two stages were used. The first was a combination of extinction and avoidance procedures to reduce the noisy responses by the children. The second was a fading technique to adjust the food preferences of the children. The program was carried out entirely by the parents; the children were never seen by E. The target behaviors were modified after 20 sessions under the two contingencies. Problems encountered while instructing the parents in behavioral techniques are discussed.

The number of techniques of behavioral control and the variety of situations in which they are applied are rapidly increasing. However, many of these situations have involved a trained professional working with a very limited population, frequently one subject. Obviously, the demand for these successful techniques is quickly outpacing the supply of personnel academically trained in these procedures. Since the implementation of these procedures is often quite simple and can be broken down into discrete segments, more attention should be given to instructing personnel not specifically trained in the use of these behavior techniques.

The existing literature shows that para-professional training has occurred with success with ward personnel in institutional settings (Allyon & Azrin, 1968;

[1]Reprinted with permission from *Psychological Reports* 28 (1971): 703-10.

115

Coleman, 1968). The education and training of teachers to be effective behavioral engineers is also an area of recent interest (Becker, Madsen, Arnold, & Thomas, 1967; Hall, Lund, & Jackson, 1968; Thomas, Becker, & Armstrong, 1968; Zimmerman & Zimmerman, 1962).

Another large area deserving attention is the training of parents to deal more effectively with the typical behavior difficulties of childhood. Inappropriate responses by the parents in the early stages of such a problem may lead to an exacerbation of an already unpleasant circumstance. Zeilberger, Sampen, and Sloane (1968) and Pendergrass (1968) report the successful training of parents to use time-out procedures in the home to stop long-standing aggressiveness and destructive behaviors in children. In other attempts to train parents in behavior management, Hawkins, *et al.* (1966) and Wahler, *et al.* (1965) used systems of signaling parents while they were engaged in actual interactions with their children.

All of the above studies have involved the therapist working in the hospital, classroom or home with the personnel to be trained in the modification procedures. Shortage of time dictates that the next step should be attempts to train these people in the complete experimental procedure from baseline through data collection in *E*'s office. This would save considerable time and allow for contact with a greater number of situations. Holland (1969) reports such a training procedure to assist parents in eliminating their son's fire-setting behavior. Holland (1970) has formulated a general guide for behavioral counseling with parents, and Hirsch and Walder (1969) have detailed their successful program for training a group of mothers in reinforcement techniques. Tharp and Wetzel (1969) have detailed an extensive program using para-professionals in a variety of natural environment situations.

The present study reports a situation similar to the cases above, the main distinguishing feature being that *E* never saw the clients. All communication about *S*s, two children aged 9 and 11 yr., was effected through the parents who were trained in a specific set of responses. The father was already in therapy with *E*, and the behavioral difficulty under consideration was a secondary problem discussed in one of the sessions.

The particular problem was the occurrence of disruptive and disturbing behaviors by the son and daughter during the dinner hour. They fussed a great deal about the foods that had been prepared. The mother, who usually spent long hours preparing special dishes and who was very concerned about the children having sufficient to eat, usually attempted some kind of coaxing and cajoling. These attempts at intervention most often resulted in increased intensity and duration of the undesirable behaviors. The reduction of time spent engaged in these inappropriate behaviors at dinner was the goal of the program.

METHOD

SUBJECTS

*S*s were siblings, a boy aged 9 and a girl aged 11. They both attended school and lived at home with their parents.

PROCEDURE

Before any program was initiated, the parents were seen together for five sessions in conjunction with the father's regular therapy appointments. During these meetings, additional background information was obtained about the children's disruptive behaviors and the parents' reactions to them. The usual target of the children's behaviors was the food prepared by the mother. She was of Spanish extraction and frequently cooked very hot and spicy dishes. This generally was the trigger for a noisy reaction on the part of one of the children. The other quickly joined the disruption once it was initiated. At this point, the behaviors became more and more aggravated, each child alternately responding to the other's behavior. The parents reported no consistency in either child starting the fussing.

The mother's typical response was one of pleading and cajoling to get the children to eat the prepared food. She frequently expressed concern about their health if they did not eat. The father reported that he was more passive in the situation until he could no longer tolerate the confusion. Then he would yell at the children and frequently leave the dinner table and seek the quiet of his den. The mother concurred with his report and expressed the wish that he would take the lead and be more active in the attempts to handle the children. It was reported that this behavior pattern had been observed for about 18 months, but it had been more severe recently.

After this information had been gathered, the parents were told of the importance of their responses to the children in maintaining the behaviors of the children. Then an over-all plan was formulated and their cooperation was assured. Since part of the plan included the possibility of the children having to leave the table before finishing the meal, the mother was initially hesitant to give her consent. The stated reason for her reluctance was concern about the children's adequate food consumption. Her reluctance was overcome when it was pointed out that under present conditions, the children were leaving a large portion of the meal because of the disturbance.

After the principles of behavior modification had been described and the specific procedures to be used fully elaborated, several hypothetical situations were developed to test the parents' responses. Consistency of response between parents was the primary concern here, since the children were in the habit of playing one parent against the other. The criterion for consistency was both parents agreeing on a specific procedure in a given situation. As will be detailed later, it was usually left to the father to intervene when a disruption occurred. The mother was to support the actions of the father.

The final step before initiating the program was several complete behavioral rehearsals of possible dinner time situations. A colleague joined E in playing the roles of the two children, and several dinner scenes with various kinds of disturbances were enacted. The parents were told to respond as they had been instructed. A videotape was taken of some of these role-playing situations to provide the parents with some feedback of their behaviors.

The proposed plan was a two-phase procedure. During the first phase, the parents were instructed to serve dinner in the usual fashion. Three days of baseline were collected. The data collected were the number of minutes of the dinner meal during which there was disturbance by the children. Included under disturbing behaviors were loud verbal exchanges between the children, screaming or crying by either child, excessive playing or manipulation of the food, and other such behaviors that generally commanded the parents' attention. Both parents were instructed to keep this time measure independently during each dinner meal. To avoid any undue attention to these recordings, time was kept by the parents' watches and kitchen clock.

After these baseline observations were collected the first contingency was introduced. If there was any disturbance, the father was to make the following statement: "Eat the food or don't eat it, but no shouting." Instead of shouting, the father could substitute whatever inappropriate behavior that was occurring at the time. If the disturbance subsided, the children were allowed to finish the meal choosing whichever foods they preferred. If the disturbances continued, the offender was sent to his room without finishing dinner. If this did happen, the mother was carefully instructed not to provide any late snack or extra-heavy breakfast. The parents continued to record the amount of time of disturbing behaviors and this procedure remained in effect till the disturbance had subsided.

A second phase of the procedure was then instituted. During this part, the mother was gradually to introduce some of the formerly non-preferred foods in increments of one tablespoon. For example, on the first night of this regimen, only one tablespoon of one non-preferred food would be placed on the plate. The contingency was that the children had to eat that food before they could go on to the other food. If they did not eat the non-preferred food, they could not continue with the dinner. The number of tablespoonfuls was gradually increased over nights with the same contingency in effect. If a meal was missed, the same cautions about late-night snacks and heavy breakfasts were observed.

During the course of the program, the parents were seen once or twice a

week to review the progress and to provide additional rehearsal of their behaviors.

RESULTS

Several explanations of the rationale supporting the procedures to be used were
required before parental cooperation was gained. Of particular concern was the
possibility of the children missing meals. After this initial period of explanatory
discussion, the contingencies were implemented.

Fig. 1 shows the results of the first contingency. During the three days of
baseline, there was an average of 34 min. of disturbance. This time approxi-
mated the duration of the meal, which was usually terminated by the father leaving the table. There was a rapid reduction in the amount of disturbance once the
first contingency was in effect. There was a drop to 18 min. the first night. By the
fifth night after baseline there was only one minute of recorded disturbance,
while the over-all length of the meal was about 40 min. The parents reported
that they were in very close agreement in their observations of disturbing behaviors. There was less than a minute variation between the times recorded for any
given meal. The data points presented are an average of the parents' two times.

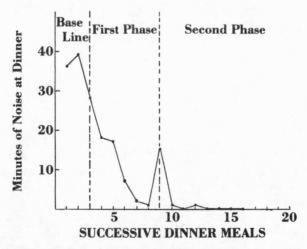

**Figure 1. Number of minutes of disturbing behaviors at dinner through
three nights of baseline and 13 nights of contingency. Each point is the
average of the observations of both parents for a given night. During the
first phase, an avoidance contingency was in effect. Previously non-
preferred foods were being faded into the dinner meal during the second
phase.**

During these first five nights after baseline, neither child was asked to leave the table despite the fact that the father had to repeat the rule several times on each of the first three nights.

On the sixth night after baseline or Day 9 of the program, the second contingency was put into effect. The initial contingency about disturbances also remained in effect. The parents continued to record the amount of disturbance until it had leveled off at a near zero level several nights later.

Table 1 shows the increases in non-preferred foods presented to and consumed by each of the children. By the twelfth day of this regime, eight tablespoons of formerly non-preferred food were being eaten. The procedure was accepted readily by the children and no meals were missed by either child. There were no additional disturbances during the second phase of the procedure.

Table 1
Amount of non-preferred food eaten during second contingency

Day of program	Day of 2nd contingency	Non-preferred foods eaten (tbs)
9	1	1
10	2	2
11	3	2
12	4	3
13	5	3
14	6	4
15	7	5
16	8	6
17	9	7
18	10	7
19	11	8
20	12	8

There was another aspect to the program which was implemented informally and for which there are no data. Once the level of disturbing behaviors was reduced to an acceptable level, the parents were encouraged to engage the children in more appropriate conversations on topics of interest. In this way the children would be receiving the attention of the parents but now for appropriate behaviors. By structuring the situation in this way, the probability of some new inappropriate attention-seeking behavior occurring was reduced. This new trend in the family conversation may have also helped to maintain an acceptable duration for the meal. In the latter stages of the second contingency the average length of the dinner meal was 45 min. If no alternative had been developed, the children might have rushed through the meal to escape the non-reinforcing situation.

DISCUSSION

This report demonstrates the alleviation of a problem situation of 18 mo. duration within a period of 20 days. The two-phase procedure made use of the techniques of extinction, avoidance and fading.

As is frequently done in such social interactions, it was hypothesized that the attention and reactions of the parents were maintaining the disturbances on the part of the children. Therefore, the first phase of the procedure was a combination of extinction and avoidance. The disturbing behaviors were given no more attention than the statement of the rule about eating or not eating but no disturbance. This rule was backed by the condition of having to leave the table if the disturbance persisted. Having to leave the table would have constituted a time-out from the social attention of the family group. This avoidance contingency was added for two reasons. First, it would provide a more rapid elimination of the undesired behaviors than simply ignoring them, and second, it allowed the father an opportunity to assert himself in the family situation. The wife had commented about his lack of participation and saw a more active role by the father as very desirable. Both parents reported that the statement of the rule by the father had a strong impact on the children. It was in sharp contrast to his usual silence and apparently increased his effectiveness judging from the rapid decline in the disturbing behaviors.

When questioned about why neither of the children was sent from the table on the first and second nights after baseline when there were 18 and 17 min. of disturbing behaviors respectively, the parents admitted that they were probably lenient and swayed by the improvement compared to the baseline nights. The only other night in which there were marked disturbances was the sixth night of the contingency or the ninth night in Fig. 1. This was the night the second contingency was introduced. It was met with an increased frequency of the disturbing behaviors, and this resulted in a brief disagreement between the parents as to whether the children should be made to leave the table. The children quickly seized this inconsistency as an opportunity to engage in the old behavior pattern. The inconsistency was resolved by the next evening and the children once again abided by the stated contingency.

There were a number of reasons for making the second phase a separate part of the procedure. It was thought that the children were not exhibiting a distaste for particular foods as much as employing an attention-seeking device. It was hoped that the food preferences would adjust congruent with the elimination of the inappropriate behaviors. This was not the case. Even with reduction of noise and disturbances, the children were still leaving some foods on their plates. This was an obvious concern to the mother. Therefore, the second strategy of fading in increasing amounts of non-preferred foods over successive evenings was implemented. Consumption of these foods by Ss once the contingency was put in effect indicates that either the behavior was performed more for attention than as a demonstration of an aversion for the particular foods or that the previously aversive foods have now become associated with positive reinforcement and this has changed the reinforcement value of these foods.

As was mentioned, the training of the parents was completed during the father's therapy sessions and in the absence of the children. Under these circumstances the development of hypothetical practice situations and role-playing assumed greater importance. It allowed the parents some practice with the responses they would have to make during the modification procedure. Production of the response in a task-oriented situation is always a better criterion of proficiency than a verbal statement indicating understanding. Also, auditory or visual feedback about these responses appears to strengthen them further.

Considerable attention has been given in this report to the results of a program implemented by parents recently trained in specific behavioral techniques. Although the situation differs in some respects from previous reports, the particular techniques employed had been effectively used in the past and the results were therefore expected.

At this stage of development of behavioral analysis, more consideration should be given to the techniques of instructing parents, teachers and others as behavior managers. Frequently such training is different from the person's usual operating procedure. It calls for viewing behavior from a different point of reference. There were some difficulties encountered in the early stages of this experiment in eliciting the cooperation of the parents. Similar problems are reported by others, e.g., Ayllon and Azrin (1968), Holland (1969). Other difficulties in the present study were getting the parents to use the time-out procedure as specified and to accept the importance of having a reversal of contingencies to specify clearly the critical stimuli in the situation. Once the behavior problem was alleviated, they were quite satisfied that the disturbing conditions had been specified and corrected. Any re-establishment of the problem behaviors would have been totally inappropriate within their frame of reference. Important information would be gathered if a systematic analysis was done on a successful shaping procedure for making someone an effective behavior modifier.

REFERENCES

Ayllon, T., & Azrin, N. H. *The token economy: motivational system for therapy and rehabilitation.* New York: Appleton-Century-Crofts, 1968.

Becker, W. C., Madsen, C. H., Jr., Arnold, R., & Thomas, D. R. The contingent use of teacher attention and praise in reducing classroom behavior problems. *Journal of Special Education,* 1967, 1, 287-307.

Coleman, A. Utilization of operant conditioning concepts and techniques for the treatment of character and behavior disorders. Paper presented at the meeting of the American Psychological Association, San Francisco, September, 1968.

Hall, R. V., Lund, D., & Jackson, D. Effects of teacher attention on study behavior. *Journal of Applied Behavior Analysis*, 1968, 1, 1-12.

Hawkins, R. P., Peterson, R. F., Schweid, D., & Bijou, S. W. Behavior therapy in the home: amelioration of problem parent-child relations with the parent in a therapeutic role. *Journal of Experimental Child Psychology*, 1966, 4, 99-107.

Hirsch, I., & Walder, L. Training mothers in groups as reinforcement therapists for their own children. *Proceedings, 77th Annual Convention, APA*, 1969, 4, 561-562.

Holland, C. J. Elimination by the parents of fire-setting behavior in a 7-yr.-old boy. *Behavior Research and Therapy*, 1969, 7, 135-137.

Holland, C. J. An interview guide for behavioral counseling with parents. *Behavior Therapy*, 1970, 1, 70-79.

Pendergrass, E. Behavior modification of autistic and retarded children using time-out procedure. Paper presented at the meeting of the American Psychological Association, San Francisco, August, 1968.

Tharp, R. G., & Wetzel, R. J. *Behavior modification in the natural environment.* New York: Academic Press, 1969.

Thomas, D. R., Becker, W. C., & Armstrong, M. Production and elimination of disruptive classroom behavior by systematically varying teacher's behavior. *Journal of Applied Behavior Analysis*, 1968, 1, 35-45.

Wahler, R. G., Winkel, G. H., Peterson, R. F., & Morrison, D. C. Mothers as behavior therapists for their own children. *Behavior Research and Therapy*, 1965, 3, 113-124.

Zeilberger, J., Sampen, S., & Sloane, H. N., Jr. Modification of a child's problem behaviors in the home with the mother as therapist. *Journal of Applied Behavior Analysis*, 1968, 1, 47-53.

Zimmerman, E. H., & Zimmerman, J. The alteration of behavior in a special classroom situation. *Journal of the Experimental Analysis of Behavior*, 1962, 5, 59-60.

Chapter 14

Behavior Modification
and the Brat Syndrome[1]
Martha E. Bernal, John S. Duryee,
Harold L. Pruett, and Beverlee J. Burns

A program of behavior modification was formulated for the purpose of train-ing a mother to control her 8 1/2-yr.-old emotionally disturbed boy who was a se-vere disciplinary problem. Training was based upon learning principles, and behavioral feedback to the mother was provided via closed circuit television. Mother-son interactions were videotaped as the mother practiced step-by-step instructions, and the interaction tapes were viewed by the mother for appraisal of her success in carrying out the instructions. Within a few weeks, the boy's abusive behavior was reduced, and treatment effects were still evident 23 weeks after initiation of the program. The roles of various factors as they con-tributed to the treatment of the brat syndrome are discussed.

The purpose of this paper is to describe a behavior modification program de-signed for one "brat." A brat will be defined as a child who often engages in tantrums, assaultiveness, threats, etc., which are highly aversive and serve to ren-der others helpless in controlling him. Collectively, such behaviors will be called "the brat syndrome" for purposes of convenience. Surveys of the relative fre-quency of presenting complaints at child guidance clinics indicate that brats, as defined above, are among the most frequent consumers of mental health ser-vices for children (Anderson & Dean, 1956; Wolff, 1961).

Within recent years, a number of papers (Boardman, 1962; Hawkins,

[1]Reprinted with permission from the *Journal of Consulting and Clinical Psychology* 32 (1968): 447-55.

125

Peterson, Schweid, & Bijou, 1966; Russo, 1964; Williams, 1959) have described the use of learning principles in the treatment of children who qualify as brats. These papers have emphasized the reprogramming of the child's social environment by providing advice or training to the parent regarding techniques for reducing the child's aversive behaviors and strengthening more acceptable ones. Underlying the emphasis on training parents as therapists is the assumption that brat behaviors are learned, and are maintained by the child's parents (Wahler, Winkel, Peterson, & Morrison, 1965).

Two major findings have resulted from previous brat research: (a) simple learning principles are extremely useful in modifying this type of behavior, and (b) parents of children who are brats are capable of changing their behavior in such a way as to take over control functions with their children. These are encouraging findings that should have broad applicability in mental health settings. However, the success of any program for modification of brat behaviors ultimately depends upon the knowledge and sophistication of the professional who designs or engineers the program. There are large variations among brats and their interpersonal environments, and these differences require tailoring of programs to the idiosyncratic features of each child-parent combination. The behavioral engineer is confronted with the task of selecting learning principles, reinforcers, parent training techniques, and therapeutic strategies as he deals with each new child. Successful performance of these tasks requires that he learn both from his own experience as well as from the experience of others. The present paper is intended as an additional source of information from which the professional may draw ideas and guidelines for designing parent training programs. The program designed for one classical brat was similar to that used by Wahler *et al.* (1965) and in addition television was used to provide behavioral feedback to the mother.

SUBJECT AND HISTORY

Jeff, age 8½ years, was referred to an outpatient psychiatric clinic because he had frequent temper tantrums and physically attacked his mother, teachers, and peers. "I have a right to do anything I want to do," as he put it, was his attitude toward life. Parental disciplinary attempts had included spanking and restriction of privileges, to no avail. An only child, he regulated family activities; for example, he dictated when his mother could sit in the living room.

Jeff was enrolled in a private school for emotionally disturbed children. In school, he was highly demanding of the teacher's attention and alternately bullied and tattled on the other children, depending upon their physical size and strength. While socially he was an ogre, academically he achieved at the fourth-grade level, and intellectually his IQ test scores ranged from 106 on the WISC

Performance Scale to 143 on the Peabody Picture Vocabulary Test. Psychiatric and psychological diagnostic opinions ranged from adjustment reaction of childhood to schizophrenia.

Jeff had many other presenting problems. He wet his bed almost every night, suffered from skin allergies, and was susceptible to frequent respiratory illnesses including pneumonia, bronchitis, and chronic asthma. He sounded as if he had memorized his lines and was delivering them in a loud, stilted, and exaggerated manner. Frequent non sequiturs and odd phrases punctuated his verbal behavior. For example, he said, "You are distracting my image" in the context of being ignored. Other peculiar actions included a relatively high rate of rocking, drawing television channel symbols, and moving his head back and forth, repetitively. His bizarreness, intellectual display of a vast vocabulary and fund of general information, and his incapacity to make or keep friends were probably sufficient reasons for the neighborhood children's shunning him. He had neither playmates at home nor allies among his schoolmates.

Jeff was a sickly child from the time he had his first asthma attack at 16 months of age. Various respiratory illnesses followed in step with recurring asthmatic episodes, and the parents began to give in to his demands for fear of precipitating or aggravating his illnesses. When he was 3 years old they enrolled him in a nursery school where he engaged in frequent rocking and temper outbursts and was a social isolate. Advice from the nursery-school teacher relating to management of Jeff's biting and hitting his mother consisted of substituting a rubber or plastic object for him to bite or a hitting bag so as to help him vent his anger. When he reached the age of 6 years, he was placed in a small private class but was withdrawn within 5 months because the faculty were not equipped to help him. Consultation with a school psychiatrist resulted in the public school system's refusal to admit him into a regular classroom. At age 7 years he was enrolled in the private school where he was attending at the time of the referral. In the school, individual psychotherapy was provided by a psychologist for about 3 months; the parents reported no improvement.

Questions regarding brain dysfunction as an explanation of Jeff's behavior disorder had been raised because he had suffered three grand mal convulsions associated with high temperatures at ages 4, 5, and 7 years. However, an electroencephalographic recording done just 3 months prior to the beginning of the present study was within normal limits, and neither neurologist nor psychologist reported evidence of major organic dysfunction.

From the time Jeff was a baby, the parents had increasing marital difficulties and each had been in intensive psychotherapy for 3 years. At the time of referral, the father was living away from home except for weekends when he slept on the living room couch in the mother's apartment. Since the strain between the parents was very evident, the first step taken prior to any therapeutic commitment was to ask the parents to tell Jeff that they were separated and to request that the father live totally separate from Jeff and his mother, maintaining visits with Jeff without the mother's presence. This request was carried out 2 months prior to the first intervention.

PART 1: JEFF AND MOTHER

The study was divided into two parts. Part 1 includes Weeks 0-13, constituting a period of time during which only Jeff and his mother were seen, and Part 2 includes Weeks 14-25, when another neighborhood child, Albert, was included in the treatment program with Jeff and his mother. Reasons for inclusion of Albert are given at the end of Part 1.

PROCEDURE

Initial interview. An initial interview was held with the parents to obtain specification of the presenting complaints. The parents agreed to permit audiotaped observations in the home and videotaped observations at the clinic. They were asked to tell Jeff that these recordings would be made in order that he and his parents might learn how to get along with each other. The mother was requested to begin keeping daily notes of conflicts with Jeff: what happened, what the child and mother did and said, and how the conflict ended. Since the father was about to move to another city temporarily, only the mother was included in treatment.

Treatment plan. During observation, it was noted that the mother had a high rate of indiscriminate response; she attended and verbally responded to him constantly in a meek, soft monotone, even when correcting him. Much of her behavior seemed to be in the class of escape and avoidance reactions, that is, she tried to pacify Jeff at all costs. For instance, if she refused to give him a snack, he would respond, "If you don't. I'll scream," or "I'll hit you," or "I'll have an asthma attack," whereupon the mother would give in. If she did not, the boy would carry out his threat. Jeff's control of his mother was so complete that she generally exerted no control functions. No expressions of warm emotional response between Jeff and his mother were noted in any of these pretreatment observations. When asked how she felt about Jeff, the mother stated that she did not like him, and was terrified of him.

The first step in training was to teach the mother to reduce her verbal output and to selectively ignore all of Jeff's abusive behaviors, from sulking to direct physical assault. This plan was intended to help her make decisions about her own behavior as she and Jeff interacted, and to extinguish his abuse.

Step 2 was to establish certain maternal behaviors as conditioned negative reinforcers by associating them with physical punishment. The behaviors or cues consisted of ignoring abuse and if ignoring did not stop it, the mother was to express anger and order him to stop. Finally, if he did not stop, she was to spank him. Hopefully, these cues, ignoring, frowning, angry tone of voice, the word "don't" etc., if clearly presented and consistently paired with punishment when the boy did not obey, would take on properties of conditioned negative reinforcers. The conditioned negative reinforcers would assume control functions when produced contingent upon the child's "bad" behavior or when removed contingent upon "good" behavior.

Several important considerations were involved in the design of instructions to the mother. She reported that, in moments of extreme frustration, she had severely spanked him. These spankings, however, were not consistently associated with cues which might serve as discriminative stimuli for the boy, as an aid in determining when his behavior would earn punishment. It was hoped that by instructing the mother on the use of punishment such severe spankings would be avoided. A second consideration was that the mother had seldom carried out her threats of punishment. The training would have to stress the reduction of threats so that when the mother said she was going to punish, punishment would follow. Unless such consistency was maintained by the mother, it seemed likely that the angry cues would fail to acquire stimulus functions.

The third step was to have the mother identify acceptable behaviors as they occurred, positively reinforce them by responding warmly and praising him, and specify to Jeff which of his behaviors were acceptable. When during positive reinforcement training, the mother responded both to his acceptable behavior and to his peculiar or "silly" talk, it became necessary to try to help her discriminate these two behavior classes, so that she would not maintain the peculiar verbalizations.

Treatment. The treatment steps were divided into five lessons, called interventions; the series of interventions was defined as treatment. Treatment of Jeff's other deviant behaviors was postponed pending establishment of maternal control.

The first videotaped session, made before any interventions occurred, was called Pretreatment. During filming of the Pretreatment and all subsequent sessions, Jeff and his mother interacted freely, and Jeff sometimes had a game to play. The mother was given specific instructions during intervention sessions. One uninstructed Posttreatment videotaped session was held approximately 11 weeks after Pretreatment.

The format of the interventions was as follows: The mother and one of the experimenters met without Jeff for 30 minutes and instructions were reviewed with her. Excerpts from the most recent videotape were played to demonstrate points at which the new operants were to be used and to identify discrepancies between her performance and any previous instructions. She and Jeff were then videotaped for approximately 15 minutes and a brief tone was played over the intercom system to cue her reinforcement of Jeff's abusive behaviors. Following the interaction, the mother was warmly praised for adequate performance. The mother's questions regarding problems arising at home were always answered by indicating that she would receive assistance only with problems occurring under observation at the clinic.

RESULTS

Videotaped interaction data. The primary method of data reduction for the interaction sessions was the time sampling technique (Arrington, 1939; Koch, 1948). Behavior categories of interest were delineated and each interaction session was divided into 30-second samples. Each first occurrence of the specified behaviors within each sample was given a time sampling score (*TSS*) of 1; additional occurrences within a sample were unscored. Thus, a maximum *TSS* of 30, representing 15 minutes of interaction time, was possible for any single session.

The scored categories were: (*a*) Jeff abuses (Jeff refuses to obey requests or commands, uses foul language, threatens, screams, bites, hits, throws objects, kicks, makes loud noises), (*b*) Jeff obeys, (*c*) mother ignores Jeff's abuse (mother does not visually attend or speak contingent upon Jeff's abuse), (*d*) mother ignores Jeff regardless of his behavior, (*e*) mother commands or requests, (*f*) mother is affectionate (mother smiles, praises, encourages, or caresses Jeff), (*g*) mother spanks Jeff.

Initially, two observers trained in scoring by going through the Pretreatment and Intervention 1 tapes three times and stopping every 30 seconds to discuss the scoring of the behavioral events; they made no scores at this time. Then they independently scored the two tapes and all other tapes except Intervention 5, viewing them once for scoring of Jeff's behaviors and again for scoring of the mother's behaviors. Proportion of agreement between observers was determined by dividing the number of agreements (both occurrence and nonoccurrence of behavior) by 30. Agreement on Jeff's behaviors ranged from .86 to 1.00 with a mean of .94. Agreement for the mother's behaviors ranged from .80 to 1.00 with a mean of .95. *TSS* data for all sessions except Interventions 4 and 5 are shown in Table 1. The general nature of instructions to the mother is written under the designated session.

During the Pretreatment session, before the mother received any instructions, she ignored only one scored occurrence or 11% of Jeff's abuse, and Jeff obeyed no commands. When instructed to ignore his abuse during Intervention 1, the mother succeeded in ignoring 100% of the scored occurrences of Jeff's abuse. She gave no commands during either Intervention 1 or 2. The instructions for Intervention 2 were designed to help her control Jeff's physical attacks on her. During this intervention, he bit her hand once and she carried out her in-

Table 1 *TSS* of mother's performance of instructions

Session and instruction	Jeff abuses	Mother ignores abuse	% abuse ignored	% of session mother ignores	Number of commands Jeff obeys	% of session mother affectionate
Pretreatment						
No instruction	9	1	11	3	0 of 4	0
Intervention 1						
Ignore abuse	13	13	100	73	—	0
Intervention 2						
Spank if he hits you	13	11	85	72	—	0
Intervention 3						
Differentiate positive and negative response	13	13	100	43	1 of 2	7
Posttreatment						
No instruction	2	2	100	7	2 of 2	20

structions. There were no other occurrences of physical attacks during Intervention 2, but she continued to ignore 85% of his abuse. It was noted that during Interventions 1 and 2 she was very successful in ignoring Jeff most of the time, whether he was being abusive or not (73% and 72% for Interventions 1 and 2, respectively). When instructed to react warmly to Jeff's acceptable behavior during Intervention 3, the mother was affectionate for the first time, but her score was only 7% for the session. Her ignoring of Jeff's abuse remained consistent (100%), and there was a drop in ignoring of Jeff during the session (43%). Results for Intervention 4 when she was asked to discriminate Jeff's acceptable verbalization from his "silly" talk will not be presented because they could not be clearly evaluated.

Intervention 5 started off with the mother immediately commanding Jeff to sit in a chair next to her. He refused, and the mother proceeded to practice her instructions. Data for the struggle that followed were obtained by using an event recorder to note covariations among the mother's actions and the time that Jeff spent sitting in the designated chair. In order to maintain chronological continuity, Intervention 5 data shown in Figure 1 will be discussed, then the reader will be referred back to Table 1. In Figure 1, the mother's commands to sit are shown as a cumulative curve, and the hatchmarks indicate when she spanked Jeff. Time throughout the 24.5 minute session is divided into consecutive 30-second intervals along the abcissa. The shaded area corresponds to the number of seconds within each interval that Jeff was seated. Four spankings were administered, and then he sat for most of the rest of the session. When he asked to

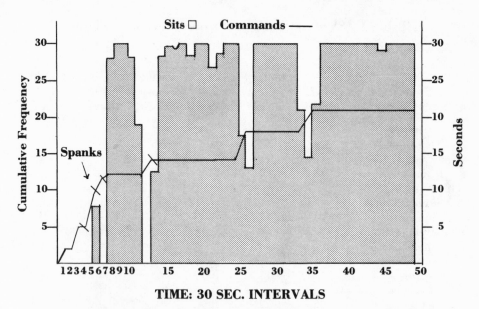

TIME: 30 SEC. INTERVALS

Figure 1. Intervention 5: Establishment of control.

get up, or actually left the chair, the mother's commands were successful in inducing him to obey. During the session, the mother's verbal and facial expressions were angry, and the boy's appreciation of her anger was expressed in his question, "Are you angry?" which he asked just after the third spanking. While he sat in the chair, he continued to swear, scream, and threaten.

The Posttreatment session followed Intervention 5; the data are shown in the last row of Table 1. The mother successfully ignored both occurrences of Jeff's abuse, but ignored him very seldom during the session (7%) while scoring higher (20%) for affectionate behavior than in previous sessions. Jeff obeyed both commands given him. Following Posttreatment it was judged no further instruction was necessary unless the mother requested it, and treatment was terminated with the understanding that she would call should there be further difficulties.

Five weeks after Intervention 5, the mother called to report that she could not manage Jeff when a normal 9½-year-old neighborhood boy, Albert, was in their home. Albert had entered Jeff's life earlier in treatment, and while there had been reports of Jeff's rudeness to Albert, those incidents were relatively mild. Coincident with the telephone call, the mother wrote in her notes that Jeff was extremely antagonistic toward Albert, and wondered if she showed "too much friendship" toward Albert in Jeff's presence. An appointment was set up for the following week.

PART 2. JEFF, ALBERT, AND MOTHER

PROCEDURE

In Jeff's presence, the mother asked Albert to join Jeff in his television program so that they might learn how to get along better. Albert probably saw the request as a service he was asked to perform in order to be of help to Jeff.

Jeff, Albert, and the mother were first videotaped on two consecutive weeks; the boys played a game and the mother was asked to proceed as if they were at home. Following the two videotapings, the tapes were studied in order to determine how to help the mother control Jeff as well as facilitate amicable play with Albert. Three major events seemed outstanding in the interactions: The mother was not carrying out her instructions, that is, she failed to ignore his abuse and her angry cues were not delivered with conviction, and she asked Albert to deal with Jeff rather than intervening directly herself, for example, she urged Albert to hit Jeff back when Jeff hit him. In addition, when Jeff continued his tantrumous behavior, the mother turned to Albert and invited him to talk and interact with her. The mother was then seen for two 1½-hour sessions; these were called Interventions 6 and 7.

Intervention 6. A lecture on basic operant principles was given the mother, with examples drawn from incidents between Jeff and herself. Instructions previously given the mother were properly labeled and reviewed.

Intervention 7. The two videotapes were reviewed, and the mother was encouraged to stop the tape and praised whenever she could formulate reasonable alternatives to her behavior. Direct intervention with Jeff was emphasized and attention was focused on the effects of her favoritism toward Albert.

On the following 2 weeks, the boys and the mother were again videotaped. She was asked to use the information imparted during Interventions 6 and 7. At no time during the four interaction sessions involving Albert was the mother cued by the tone.

RESULTS

Videotaped interaction data. Data for the four sessions were reduced as in Part 1. The first of the four videotapes was first viewed twice by the observers and discussed in order to arrive at a consensus on the definition of the new behavior categories. Interobserver agreement ranged from 82% to 100% with means of 92%, 94%, 95%, and 99% for Sessions 1-4, respectively.

The following categories were scored: (*a*) Jeff abuses mother or Albert (defined as in Part 1), (*b*) Jeff speaks in a soft voice (Jeff's speech is clearly characterized as "nice," and tone of voice is at normal conversational level), (*c*) Jeff breaks rules (Jeff refuses to play by the rules of the game or the conditions speci-

Table 2 *TSS* of Jeff's behaviors with Albert and mother

Session	Abuses mother	Abuses Albert	Soft voice	Breaks rules	Plays amicably
Pretreatment 1	26	11	2	7	0
Pretreatment 2	1	2	0	7	7
Posttreatment 1	1	0	27	1	27
Posttreatment 2	0	0	30	0	28

fied by Albert or mother), (*d*) amicable play (Jeff and Albert play a game in a friendly manner, with no incident of conflict between the two).

Time sampling data are displayed in Table 2; the two interactions before Interventions 6 and 7 are designated Pretreatments 1 and 2, and Posttreatment sessions 1 and 2 occurred following instruction of the mother. Comparison of Pretreatment and Posttreatment sessions shows improvement in all categories.

Mother's notes and other observations. The mother's notes of conflicts between herself and Jeff at home were divided into weeks, beginning on a Wednesday, when interventions were scheduled. Two research assistants who had no knowledge of interventions performed independently scored two event classes: *general abuse*, which included profanity, refusal to obey, sulking, rudeness, demands, whining, and threats, and *physical abuse*, which included hitting, biting, kicking, screaming, tantrums, and throwing things. The mother described incidents occurring at different times of the day, and within each incident the exact number of occurrences of abuse could not be determined, therefore, only first occurrences of behavior for each incident were scored. Thus, the frequency scores are underestimations of abusive occurrences. Pearson product-moment correlations between scorers were .97 for general abuse and .98 for physical abuse. The frequencies for the two event classes per week were divided by the number of days during which the boy was with his mother (he spent some weekdays and weekends with his father) to obtain rate of daily occurrences per week. Figure 2 displays the rates of abuse over a period of 25 weeks. Interventions are noted under the abscissa. The figure shows that a sharp reduction in general abuse occurred beginning with the first intervention, and that at no time during subsequent weeks was the rate of general abuse comparable to the pretreatment weeks.

During Week 3, when the mother was instructed to begin ignoring the boy's abuse, an increase in physical abuse occurred. On Week 4, following Intervention 2 wherein the mother was instructed in control of the boy's physical attacks, a drop in this form of abuse occurred, and its rate in subsequent weeks was below the mean level of the first 3 weeks, reaching a zero level by the last 5 weeks.

Validation of problems with Jeff and Albert can be seen during Week 14 where the general abuse rate shows a sharp rise. Finally, Jeff was generally abusive only eight times during the last 5 weeks of the project; such an approxi-

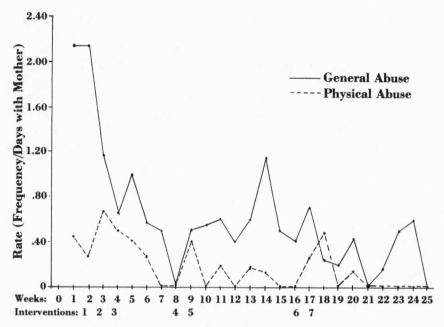

Figure 2. Jeff's abuse at home.

mate rate might be considered comparable to that of the average child who from time to time becomes difficult, but is not unmanageable.

The mother's notes suggested that much of her control was acquired through establishment of cues denoting anger as conditioned negative reinforcers. In support of this conclusion is the tally of the number of spankings administered by the mother; she spanked him four times at the clinic during Intervention 5, and then reported only nine more spankings. The effectiveness of her anger was apparent by Week 10, when she reported:

I had occasion to speak harshly to Jeff, and now he asks "How do you feel?" If I say angry he is given an explanation if he asks why, but he knows. Together with ignoring him, showing him I'm really angry by voice is working quite well. He mumbles under his breath and occasionally there is a bad word, but he responds within a reasonable time. No swats necessary.

Improvement in the relationship was gradual; there was much "testing" of the mother's authority during and after treatment. Confronted with his tyrannical behavior, she had to practice her instructions as best she could, varying them to meet the situation. The following note from Week 14 demonstrates a typical exchange:

On the freeway, I started to sing to myself. Jeff told me to stop, as he always has, and to turn off the radio. I realized I was being ordered by my child, so I told him, loudly, firmly, and without misunderstanding that I would sing any-time I felt like it. Instant tantrum. I ignored him and continued humming. He begged me to stop, and finally asked. "Why can't you stop when I tell you?" I said because I was the boss and if I felt like doing something, I would. No argu-ment, he calmed down and asked for donuts at the drivein. I stopped and we got a different order from the last time. He questioned the selection, but didn't argue or pout. "Okay, mother, whatever you feel like," he said. I very nearly choked.

Her success in controlling him in spite of his tantrums and pleas, his positive re-sponse to her firmness, and praise from relatives and friends probably served to strengthen her new reactions to him. Each test with which Jeff confronted her could be regarded as a learning trial for both of them.

Change in the mother was very apparent and could best be typified as an in-crease in assertiveness and self-esteem in her relations with others and confi-dence in her role as mother. Her increased assertiveness may well have been ini-tiated by the impact of watching herself on television with Jeff for the first time; her terse comment, "What a dishrag!" expressed its impact upon her.

Freed of her terror of the boy, she gradually grew to like him, and he in turn began to express affection. During Week 18 the following occurred after Jeff had gone to bed:

He asked to talk to me. He asked if he could take piano lessons. I told him he had a bigger project first—learning to get along with others, including chil-dren—and in a few years perhaps he could take lessons. As I went out the door he said, "I love you." I replied the same and told him how pleased I was with him. After the door was closed I heard him say to himself, "She's swell! I feel great!"

In contrast to the positive changes in Jeff and his mother, there was no evident reduction of the other presenting complaints except for the enuresis problem. Just after Intervention 2, he stopped wetting himself, and only one further wet-ting incident occurred 15 weeks later. So far as could be determined without the aid of records, the other presenting complaints did not intensify.

DISCUSSION

The treatment program designed for Jeff was successful in establishing maternal control over a period of 25 weeks. The design of the study did not provide for evaluation of the generalization of treatment effects to persons other than the mother.

A number of factors probably contributed to the effectiveness of the program. As Hawkins et al. (1966) have noted, a cooperative parent is critical for successful training. Jeff's mother's cooperation was evident in willingness to follow instructions, the voluminous notes she wrote, and a record of no appointments missed. Lang (1966) pointed up the desirability of providing some record of progress, or feedback, during training of social agents as reinforcers. Such feedback to Jeff's mother was provided by television replay, the tone cue, and friends and relatives. Two patient variables were probably important. Jeff was an only child, and lived alone with his mother. There was no one in the home regularly to interfere with her new role as the major disciplinary agent in his life. Additionally, Jeff's rate of problem behavior upon which the treatment focused was high both in the television studio and at home. Its high rate permitted a large number of occasions for modification. It is conceivable that some brats would behave very well in the clinic or television studio while being intolerable at home. In such a case, techniques such as those developed by Hawkins et al. (1966) for training the parent at home may be more useful than those described here. Finally, television provided a record of interactions that was immediately replayable. The recordings permitted very careful assessment of ongoing events and consequently facilitated tailoring of the program to the uniqueness of the relationship as it was originally and as it changed during treatment.

One unique feature of parent training programs deserves comment. It seems unnecessary to blame a mother for her childrearing mistakes without the offer of some alternative as to what she can do that is helpful. Training the parent to respond in new ways to her child emphasizes the parent's successes and minimizes dwelling upon previous mistakes or the parent's psychodynamic structure as explanations for problem behaviors. In the design of the present program, it was considered most useful and humane to phrase the instructions in terms of what she could do to help her child and to strongly emphasize correct performance. This plan was particularly pertinent during the initial stages of training, when she was struggling to deal with a child who terrified her. Later on, when she had difficulty in handling Jeff in Albert's presence, it was judged that she had experienced enough success to permit more extensive discussion of her errors, as, for example, when she was asking Albert to discipline Jeff. On occasion, she expressed her regrets regarding the manner in which she had raised Jeff. Typically, these comments received the response that what had happened before was in the past and that now she was dealing with him in a constructive manner.

REFERENCES

Anderson, F. N., & Dean, H. C. Some aspects of child guidance clinic intake policy and practices. *Public Health Monograph*, 1956, 42, 1-16.

Arrington, R. E. Time-sampling studies of child behavior. *Psychological Monographs*, 1939, 51(2, Whole No. 228).

Boardman, W. K. Rusty: A brief behavior disorder. *Journal of Consulting Psychology*, 1962, 26, 293-297.

Hawkins, R. P., Peterson, R. F., Schweid, E., & Bijou, S. W. Behavior therapy in the home: Amelioration of problem parent-child relations with the parent in a therapeutic role. *Journal of Experimental Child Psychology*, 1966, 4, 99-107.

Koch, H. M. Methods of studying the behavior and development of young children. In T. G. Andrews (Ed.), *Methods of psychology*, New York: Wiley, 1948.

Lang, P. F. The transfer of treatment. *Journal of Consulting Psychology*, 1966, 30, 373-378.

Russo, S. Adaptations in behavioural therapy with children. *Behaviour Research and Therapy*, 1964, 2, 43-47.

Wahler, G., Winkel, G. H., Peterson, R. F., & Morrison, D. C. Mothers as behavior therapists for their own children. *Behaviour Research and Therapy*, 1965, 3, 113-124.

Williams, C. D. The elimination of tantrum behavior by extinction procedures: Case report. *Journal of Abnormal and Social Psychology*, 1959, 59, 269.

Wolff, S. Symptomatology and outcome of preschool children with behavior disorders attending a child guidance clinic. *Journal of Child Psychology and Psychiatry*, 1961, 2, 269-276.

Glossary

Attention—when the reinforcement consists of paying attention—looking at, talking to—to a child.

Avoidance learning—if a certain behavior prevents a child from receiving an aversive stimulus, that behavior will be maintained.

Chaining—when two or more behaviors are put together to make up a more complex behavior, e.g., proper use of arms and legs together for swimming.

Concept formation—the learning of an abstract dimension such as large, hard, left and so forth.

Conditioned stimulus—if a stimulus is paired with a tangible stimulus, over time it will come to have the same effect on behavior as the tangible stimulus.

Contracting—where a precise agreement is made which states that if a certain behavior takes place then a particular reinforcement will be forthcoming.

Deprivation—when certain reinforcers are withheld from a child, e.g., no candy is given.

Diary-recording method—where a person records, in a narrative objective fashion, the behavior of a child. From such a diary one can find the frequency of behavior.

Discrimination—the ability to differentiate between two stimuli, e.g., the larger, the red one, the one on the left, and so forth.

Escape learning—if a certain behavior causes a child to escape an aversive stimulus, that behavior will be learned and maintained.

Event recorder—an apparatus that indicates when a behavior is taking place and when it is not.

139

Extinction—if a behavior is being reinforced, it can be reduced in frequency if the re-inforcement is removed. The behavior will then decrease in frequency.

Fading—if a parent initially aids a child with a behavior and later does it less and less, while the child does more and more, fading has taken place.

Fixed-interval schedule—when a reinforcement is only given after a certain period of time following a behavior, the child is on a fixed-interval schedule.

Fixed-ratio schedule—when a reinforcer is given after a certain number of behaviors have been performed. This number stays the same and hence is fixed.

Imitation—one way of learning a new behavior. It consists of behaving as someone else has behaved.

Incompatible behavior—when one behavior (usually undesirable) cannot be per-formed because the child is being reinforced for some other behavior.

Maintenance—the process by which a behavior continues to be performed with little attention or reinforcement given by a parent.

Modeling—*see* Imitation.

Negative reinforcement—when, by performing some behavior, one can avoid or escape some aversive stimulus. This behavior will then increase in frequency.

Operant behavior—behaviors that change the environment for a child. If the behaviors are reinforced, they will increase in frequency.

Positive reinforcement—the following of some behavior with a consequence. After a number of pairings, there will be an increase in frequency of that behavior.

Punishment—the following of some behavior with an aversive consequence. There will be a decrease in the frequency of that behavior.

Respondent—behavior that results from the application of certain stimuli (e.g., heat causes perspiration). Respondent behavior is contrasted with operant behavior.

Satiation—when so much positive reinforcement (e.g., candy) has been given that the reinforcer is no longer effective.

Shaping—the situation in which the child is reinforced for small steps that more and more closely approximate the ultimate desired behavior.

Stimulus control—where behavior is viewed as being responsive to particular di-mensions of a certain stimulus, similar to Discrimination.

Successive approximation—same as Shaping.

Tally-recording method—a way of recording behavior. A mark is made each time a behavior takes place.

Tangible reinforcer—reinforcers that can be seen or felt like candy, toys, clothes.

Time-block recording method—a way of recording behavior. If the behavior takes place during a certain period of time, a mark so indicating is made in a particular block. The block represents a certain period of time.

Time-out procedures—when the child is isolated from positive reinforcement. Used to reduce the frequency of undesirable behaviors.

Token reinforcers—reinforcers which represent some other reinforcement. Money is a token reinforcer as it can be used to purchase other reinforcers.

Variable-interval schedule—when a reinforcer is given after a certain period of time has elapsed. This period of time varies between responses in contrast to fixed-inter-val schedule.

Variable-ratio schedule—when a reinforcer is given after a certain number of responses have been performed (the number of responses required varies between responses in contrast to fixed-ratio schedule).

Verbal reinforcer—when the reinforcement is verbal praise such as "good boy" or "bad girl."

References

Ginnott, H. *Between parent and child*. New York: Macmillan Co., 1965

Homme, L. *How to use the contingency contracting in the classroom*. Urbana, Illinois: Research Press, 1969.

Wolking, W. *Behavior modification*. Paper presented at the Maryland Psychological Association Meeting, 1968.

Suggested Reading

Becker, W. C. *Parents are teachers*. Champaign, Illinois: Research Press, 1971.

Bijou, S. W. and Baer, D. M. *Child development: readings in experimental analysis*. New York: Appleton Century Crofts, 1967.

Hall, R. V. *Managing behavior*. Parts I, II, III. Lawrence, Kansas: H and H Enterprises, Inc., 1970.

Krumboltz, J. D. and Krumboltz, H. B. *Changing child's behavior*. Englewood Cliffs, New Jersey: Prentice Hall, 1972.

McIntire, R. M. *Child psychology: A behavioral approach to family problems*. Kalamazoo: Behaviordelia, 1975.

Patterson, G. R. and Gullion, M. E. *Living with children*. Champaign, Illinois: Research Press, 1968.

Ulrich, R., Stacknik, T., Mabry, J. *Control of human behavior*. Glenview, Illinois: Scott, Foresman and Co., 1966.

Ulrich, R., Stacknik, T., Mabry, J. *Control of human behavior*, Vol. 2. Glenview, Illinois: Scott, Foresman and Co., 1970.

Williams, D. L. and Jaffa, E. B. *Ice cream, poker chips and very goods*. College Park, Maryland: Distributed by the Maryland Book Exchange, 1971.

Index

147

UNIVERSITY OF MARYLAND
University Counseling Center
Shoemaker Building
College Park, Maryland 20742